ROTATION

THE ILLUSTRATED ENCYCLOPEDIA OF THE
INCAS

THE ILLUSTRATED ENCYCLOPEDIA OF THE
INCAS

The history, legends, myths and culture of the ancient native peoples of the
Andes, with over 500 photographs, maps, artworks and fine art images

DR DAVID M JONES

LORENZ BOOKS

CONTENTS

INTRODUCTION

When Francisco Pizarro and the Spanish conquistadors arrived in the Andes in 1532 they found a civilization of great sophistication and wealth. Well-planned cities with storehouses and complex ceremonial architecture, irrigated lands and an established system of agriculture, transport and communication routes, and an organized, hierarchical society were all signs of an intelligent and civilized people. Starting from the Cuzco Valley, the Incas had gradually expanded their power to form an empire, conquering and integrating land and settlements from the coastal plains inland to the rainforest. From its early roots it had developed from small farming villages to large cities with sophisticated forms of organization.

Below: A Middle Horizon bridge-spout effigy vessel from Tiwanaku with distinctive jaguar coat. Jaguars were revered by sierra cultures.

Yet despite these momentous achievements, the Incas' reign lasted less than 100 years. To understand how the Incas rose from around 40,000 people to form the largest empire in South America, we need to understand the land they lived in, their way of life, their conquests and spread of influence and, perhaps more than anything else, their religion and myths, for these lay behind so many aspects of Inca life and influenced everything from agriculture to temple building.

ANDEAN CIVILIZATION

South America comprises many dramatically different geological areas. From high Altiplanos to low coastal valleys, from lush, dense rainforest to dry, barren deserts, each landscape offers different rewards and challenges and shapes the lifestyles of its inhabitants. Such differences, and the geographical isolation of many settlements, led to different peoples in South America developing at different paces. At the same time, however, cultures in various large areas were aware of each other, and they developed links through trade, political alliance, conquest and the diffusion of ideas through direct or indirect contact.

Ancient South American cultures that can be described as 'civilizations' were confined to the Andes mountains and nearby western coastal valleys and deserts. Elsewhere, South American peoples did develop quite sophisticated societies and beliefs.

Above: Descending the Inca Trail from the Second Pass, the walker approaches the ridge-top ruins of the Sayaqmarka compound.

However, they did not build monumental ceremonial centres or cities, or develop technology of quite the same level of complexity as the Andean kingdoms and empires, and are therefore not defined as 'civilizations'.

This book concentrates on the 'Andean Area', where civilizations evolved in the sierras and adjacent foothills and coastal regions, north to south from the Colombian–Ecuadorian border to the northern half of Chile and east to west from the Amazonian Rainforest to the Pacific coast. City-states, kingdoms and empires evolved in this area, based on maize and potato agriculture and the herding of llamas, alpacas and vicuñas. The concentration of civilization in the Andean Area was due in part to the geography of the region. Within a relatively small area there is a range of contrasting landscapes, from Pacific ocean-bound coastal plains and deserts, to coastal and foothill valleys, to high mountain valleys and plateaux, to the eastern slopes running down to the edges of the rainforests and high pampas of Argentina.

A key factor in the development and endurance of these civilizations was access to and control of water, which became

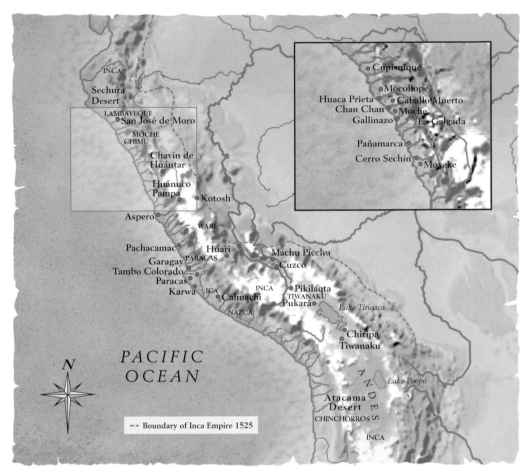

important not only functionally but also symbolically and religiously. Water was essential for agriculture, and people in naturally dry regions developed a sophisticated form of agriculture based on complex irrigation technologies, often combined with land terracing. As a result, a wide variety of crops was grown in both lowland and highland regions, which led to the development of trade between the two. The development of agriculture and trade led to different cultures specializing in different products – and not only essentials such as food but increasingly non-essential items such as ceramics and items with religious significance. As a result, these cultures developed into complex and orderly societies with sophisticated religious beliefs and structures. Thus empires are born.

SOURCES OF INFORMATION

Our knowledge of the Incas (and other South American peoples) comes from a variety of sources: from the Inca record-keepers themselves (both the *amautas* and

Below: Reed fishing boats and huts on Lake Titicaca, between Peru and Bolivia. Such vessels and materials are still used today.

the *quipucamayoqs*), from contemporary Spanish accounts and from archaeological investigations, both recent and in the past. All give us fascinating insights into a rich and colourful civilization with legendary rulers, a civil war, sacred places, mystical lines and images in the desert, imposing temples and evocative symbols, and a literal belief that the Incas will one day return to power.

REMAINS OF EMPIRES

The buildings constructed by the cult of Chávin de Huántar in the Early Horizon, the Wari and Tiwanaku empires in the Middle Horizon and the Incas in the Late Horizon can be seen and marvelled at today, along with other remains from the Andean Area. Such remains help us to understand the architectural and engineering skills of the various peoples, their social organization, their main forms of occupation and trade, and their religions.

Chávin de Huántar was a pilgrimage centre, established *c.*900BC as a U-shaped centre (others include La Galgada and Sechín Alto, both built in the Preceramic Period). Its remains show a labyrinth of passages and galleries.

Above: General map of the Inca Empire and important sites, showing how the empire stretched the length of the Andes Mountains.

Other fantastic pre-Inca sites are the Gateway of the Sun at the Tiwanaku Akapana Temple; the Paracas Cavernas cemetery, known for its desiccated mummies; the Moche centre of Cerro Blanco, where two large ceremonial platforms – the Huacas del Sol and de la Luna – were built; and the Late Intermediate Period Chimú city of Chan Chan, which comprised a complex of compounds (*ciudadelas*) containing residences for the reigning king and earlier deceased kings.

Famous remains from the Incas themselves include the city of Cuzco, the 'navel of the world', rebuilt in the plan of a crouching puma, and site of the Coricancha Temple; Huánuco Pampa, a seat of provincial admininstration; and the dramatically sited hilltop sacred city of Machu Picchu, a massive landmark on the Inca Trail. In addition, Inca engineers constructed an impressive array of roads and bridges, as well as enabling land to be developed for farming through the construction of terraces and irrigation canals.

ANDEAN RELIGION

The legends and myths of the Andean peoples, together with the remains found by archaeologists, constitute a record of ancient Andean religious belief.

Religious beliefs and deities were intimately linked with the forces of nature. Ancient South American peoples felt compelled to explain the important things in their universe, beginning with where they came from and their place in the larger scheme of things. To do this they developed accounts of what they could see in the sky and in the surrounding landscape to help them understand which things were important, and how and why this was so. Thus, the Inca god Inti belonged to the life-giving force of the sun, and Lake Titicaca, the most sacred of waters, was seen as the origin of life.

The explanatory accounts of these concepts provided a framework for living and for understanding and relating to the mysteries of the world.

COMMON BELIEFS AND IMAGERY

There were long sequences of traditional development among Andean and western coastal peoples and cultures, helped by trading and social relationships between the two. Many deities were almost universal, although given different names by different cultures, but some were individual and distinct, belonging to particular peoples and civilizations.

Above: Cotton-embroidered textile from the Early Horizon Paracas culture, with a figure reminiscent of the Chavin Staff Deity.

Nevertheless, long-standing places of ritual pilgrimage linked areas and regions and persisted despite the rise and fall of kingdoms and empires. The site and oracle of coastal Pachacamac, for example, had such potency and precedence that even the Incas recognized and revered it, although they felt compelled to establish their imperial authority by building a temple to the sun god Inti in its shadow.

Common threads run through the mythologies of Andean Area civilization and its cultures. Today's modern division of religion and politics was unknown then, at a time when the entire basis of political power was derived from divine development and designation. In Inca society, and probably in Chimú and Moche and other cultures before them, rulers and priests were often one and the same. The Inca ruler himself was regarded

Left: Gold hammered sheet-metal sun figure from Tiwanaku. The rayed head is reminiscent of the Gateway of the Sun.

as the living divine representative of Inti. Although each had specific roles, rulers and priests were intimately entwined in ruling and regulating every aspect of daily life. Ruler worship was carried beyond death through continuing ritual with the mummies of past Incas.

The landscape itself was considered sacred. Numerous natural features were regarded as semi-divine; ceremonial centres were constructed to represent myth; and ritual pathways were made across long distances, such as Nazca geoglyphic or Inca *ceque* routes.

There were many common religious elements among ancient Andean cultures, some of them almost universal, some more regional. In most regions, for example, there was a named creator god. During the later stages of Andean civilization – the Late Intermediate Period

and Late Horizon – Viracocha, with many variations, was the creator god, especially among the sierra cultures and many coastal cultures. Along the central and southern Peruvian coast there was also a certain confusion and/or rivalry with the supreme god Pachacamac. Prototypes of the creator god Viracocha are apparent in the architectural and artistic imagery of earlier civilizations.

Religious imagery throughout the Andean Area was profoundly influenced from the earliest times by rainforest animals (jaguars, serpents and other reptiles, monkeys, birds) and included composite humanoid beings. In particular, both Andean civilizations and Amazonian cultures share a fascination with the power and influence of jaguars and other large felines, such as pumas. Among symbolic motifs that persisted through the different cultures of the Andean Area, in addition to the jaguar, were feline-human hybrids, staff deities (often with a composite feline face and human body), winged beings, and falcon- or other bird-headed warriors.

ANDEAN THEMES

Several common themes pervade Andean Area religion. As well as the creator Viracocha, almost all ritual had a calendrical organization. There was a calendar based on the movements of heavenly

Left: Nazca geoglyph forming a monkey in the desert of southern Peru. Such animals figure frequently in desert coastal cultures.

bodies, including solar solstices and equinoxes, lunar phases, the synodical cycle of Venus, the rising and setting of the Pleiades, the rotational inclinations of the Milky Way and the presence within the Milky Way of 'dark cloud constellations' (stellar voids). Consultation of auguries concerning these movements was considered vital at momentous times of the year, including planting, the harvest and the start of the ocean fishing season.

Sacrifice, both human and animal, and a variety of offerings were other common practices. A fifth, extremely important and ancient theme was the assignment of sacredness to special places, called *huacas*, which could be either natural or man-made. Most of them continued to be revered despite the rise and fall of political power. Another widespread trait was the use of hallucinogenic and other drugs, especially coca and the buds of several cacti, in rituals connected to war and sacrifice. Yet another common practice was ancestor reverence and worship, charged with its own special ritual and governed by the cyclical calendar. The mummified remains of ancestors were carefully kept in special buildings or chambers, or in caves, and brought out on ritual occasions.

It is this diversity, imaginative invention and richness of expression and depiction, as well as its 'alien' appeal – at least to Western readers – that makes the religion/mythology of Andean civilization so fascinating.

Below: Chinchorros mummies, c.5000BC, in the Atacama Desert are the world's earliest known deliberate mummifications.

DISCOVERING THE INCAS AND THEIR PAST

Unlike many other ancient civilizations worldwide, none of the Andean peoples invented an alphabet or any other form of writing. As a result, the first accounts of any ancient Andean culture or history were written by Spanish conquistadors, then later by 16th- and 17th-century Spanish chroniclers.

The conquistadors related what they observed on discovering the Incas, while later chroniclers recorded accounts of the empire, its people and culture. They used two sources of information for their records: *quipucamayoqs* and *amautas*. The first were people who devised the 'writing' system of knots known as *quipus*, which involved coloured cords tied into bundles with knots, while the second were court historians responsible for learning and relating details of their culture. Interpreting these accounts was not aided by the fact that many hundreds of languages and dialects existed at that time, although one language, Quechua, dominated.

During the 19th century, more was learned about Inca and pre-Inca civilizations from the studies and collections carried out by explorers and naturalists in the earliest excavations. Further additions to our knowledge come from the results and interpretations of 20th- and 21st-century archaeological discoveries, including that of the Inca sacred city of Machu Picchu.

Left: Shadows and light on the walls of the Sacsahuaman temple mimic the lighting on the sacred landscape that lies behind it.

THE SPANISH EXPLORATIONS

Europeans first discovered the New World ('Vinland') as early as AD986, although at that time they were unaware of the vastness of its lands. However, the settlement made there was all but forgotten by Europeans by the time Christopher Columbus and others began to explore across the Atlantic in the late 15th and early 16th centuries.

THE ARRIVAL OF THE SPANISH
After explorations from Hispaniola (modern Haiti and the Dominican Republic), during 1504–9, Spaniards established the first permanent occupation of Tierra Firme (the South American mainland) in Panama in 1509. From the isthmus, Francisco Pizarro and others explored and eventually conquered the vast Inca Empire of the Andes in 1533.

Their descriptions of the peoples and cultures they found formed the opinions of Europeans towards the new worlds they had 'discovered', and enhanced convictions already formed about the natives

Below: Atahualpa, the last Inca emperor, was engaged in a bitter civil war when Pizarro landed on the northern coast of the empire.

Above: Early 16th-century Spanish caravels were the type of ships used by the explorers and conquistadors.

of the Caribbean islands. When Pizarro led his first expedition to Tierra Firme in 1524, the Aztec Empire had already been conquered by Hernán Cortés. (The reality that Columbus had not reached China but had found an unsuspected and unknown New World had become common knowledge.) Spaniards were sure that other vast empires and rich cities were there for the taking, and set out to conquer and exploit the wealth of these places for their own glory and enrichment.

With their belief that they were a superior race with a righteous duty to convert the 'heathens' they found to Christianity, to rule them and to exploit them, few Spaniards had any desire to engage with these civilizations.

A MAN WITH AMBITIONS
Pizarro made three expeditions: 1524–5, 1526–7 and 1531–3. In the first he only barely penetrated the coast of Colombia, but in the second he marched farther inland and sent his ship captain, Bartholomew Ruíz, down the coast.

Pizarro met with a mixed reception but soon began to collect gold and silver objects, and to hear tales of vast cities and riches to the south. Ruíz brought back tales of many sightings of increasing population and civilization, and no apparent hostility or fear. Moreover, he encountered a balsa trading raft well out to sea laden with gold and silver objects, elaborate textiles and two traders from the Inca subject port of Tumbes, whom he brought to Pizarro along with the gold, silver and cloth. From these two men the Spaniards learned of fabulous Inca cities, palaces, llama flocks and endless stores of gold and silver objects.

Sufficient gold and silver was taken back to Spain to whet the appetite of the Spanish crown and to interest enough adventurers to raise funds to send a third expedition, this time into the Andes, with the purpose of conquest and conversion.

The Inca Empire discovered by Pizarro was at its greatest expansion, but had only recently itself conquered the kingdoms and peoples of the northern Andes and coasts of modern Ecuador and central Colombia. Nevertheless, Pizarro's chroniclers describe vast wealth in gold and silver objects, rich textiles, neatly laid-out cities and storehouses full of produce and other goods. There were masonry walls and fortresses of blocks so well fitted together that no mortar was needed, lands with irrigation systems and sophisticated agriculture and herds of 'sheep' (llamas). Balsa rafts traded up and down the coasts, while transport and communication were facilitated by a network of smooth roads and bridges along the coasts, across rivers and into the high mountains.

SMALLPOX AND CIVIL WAR

The Spaniards also found an empire in trouble, partly, although unknowingly, of their own doing. Ironically, smallpox, introduced into mainland America by the

Below: Francisco Pizarro and Diego de Almagro, his ambitious accomplice, as depicted by Guaman Poma de Ayala.

Spaniards in their conquest of the Aztecs, spread rapidly south from Mesoamerica, infecting the last conquering Sapa Inca (emperor), Huayna Capac (1493–1526), along with his heir apparent. As he became ill, Huayna Capac received reports from traders from the northern reaches of his empire of bearded strangers who sailed in strange ships. These reports coincided with a series of ill omens, and his priests prophesied evil and disaster when they witnessed the death of an eagle, which fell out of the sky after being mobbed by buzzards, during ceremonies in honour of the sun god Inti.

When Capac died, his son Huáscar seized the throne but was challenged by another son, Atahualpa, who commanded the Inca armies and marched from the

Above: Francisco Pizarro of Trujillo, of Estremadura, Spain (1475–1541), conqueror of the Incas.

northernmost province of Quito. The Inca court split into two supporting factions and civil war raged for six years. At the time of Pizarro's arrival at Tumbes on the coast of Quito province in 1532, Atahualpa's generals had only recently defeated Huáscar's army at the Inca capital, Cuzco, and captured his brother to secure the throne. The disruption caused by the civil war had weakened the Inca Empire's cohesion. As in Cortés' conquest of the Aztecs, Pizarro was able to exploit the ill omens prophesied by the Inca priesthood, which had created misgivings among the Incas.

CHRONICLERS AND INFORMANTS

From the earliest explorations of Tierra Firme, chroniclers among the conquistadors left descriptions of the peoples they encountered. Later, historians in the 16th and 17th centuries wrote accounts of the Inca Empire and its past and descriptions of Inca culture and other peoples. Even so, the lack of a written language among any of the Andean Area civilizations before the Spanish conquest necessitates that these descriptions of Inca history and religion be complemented with archaeological, artistic and architectural images and evidence, particularly for pre-Inca cultures.

KNOT HISTORIES
Although no Andean culture developed a writing system, the recording device known as the *quipu*, a system of tied bundles of string with distinctive knotting and dyed colours, served as an *aide-mémoire* to designated *quipucamay-*

Below: Felipe Guaman Poma de Ayala travelling in Peru. He chronicled the conquest of the Inca Empire and Inca life and culture.

Above: The quipu, *a device of knotted and dyed cotton and wool string, was used by special court officials to keep records.*

oqs (literally 'knot makers'). Many of the first records of Inca culture transcribed by Spanish priests were based on the memories of *quipucamayoqs* and their recitals of Inca accounts and records, religious concepts and beliefs, and history.

For example, in the 1560s and 1570s the Spaniard Sarmiento de Gamboa, who was given the task of recording Inca history by the fourth Viceroy of Peru, Francisco de Toledo, claimed to have interviewed more than 100 *quipucamayoqs*, 42 of whom he actually names.

Colleagues of the *quipucamayoqs* were the *amautas* – officially appointed court philosophers and historians. They were responsible for memorizing, recounting, interpreting, reinterpreting, amplifying, reciting and passing on to successors the legends and history, family trees and special events of the Inca kings and queens. They therefore became another principal source of Inca history, legend, religious belief and social organization, and in this way were invaluable not only to the early Spanish chroniclers but also to colonial officials struggling to implement Spanish administration and to collect produce and

taxes. The *amautas'* detailed knowledge of the Inca *ayllu* (kinship), *mitamaes* (redistributed peoples) and *mit'a* (labour service) helped the Spaniards to take advantage of and adapt a system of obligations that was already in place.

INTERPRETING SOURCES
There was a danger, however, of taking such sources too literally, and of having to cope with the problems of conflicting accounts. Spanish chroniclers' and Catholic priests' transcriptions of the descriptions of Inca history and culture by *quipucamayoqs* and *amautas* were fraught with opportunities for misinterpretation. Deliberately or accidentally omitting some facts, embellishing others, and amending and reinterpreting what they had been told meant events could be retold to suit a particular bias. The resulting conflicting versions could be used to argue a particular legal claim or to justify a particular Spanish action or exploitative practice.

Nevertheless, the descriptions of Inca societies contained in these early records provide an invaluable source of information on Inca culture that can help make sense of archaeological evidence and vice versa.

SPANISH CHRONICLERS

About two dozen chroniclers' works provide information on the Incas and their contemporaries. Chief among them are the following writings. The mid-16th-century author Cieza de León's *Crónica del Peru* (1553 and 1554) contains much on Inca myth, while Juan de Betanzos' *Narrative of the Incas* (1557) recorded the subject from the point of view of the Inca nobility. Another record of Inca mythology is provided by Garcilasco de la Vega's (known as 'El Inca') *Comentarios Reales de los Incas* (1609–17), a comprehensive history of the Inca Empire.

The *Relación de los Quipucamayoqs* (written in Spain in 1608) comprises materials assembled to support the claims of a hopeful late pretender to the Inca throne, one Melchior Carlos Inca. He attempted to add depth and weight to his legitimacy by incorporating a version of the early foundation of Cuzco and the origin myth of the Incas, using as his source the manuscript of an inquest that had been held in 1542, the informants at which were four elderly *quipucamayoqs* who had served the Inca before the Spanish conquest.

Outside Cuzco, several sources provide accounts of myths from the regions of the empire. The exceptionally important Huarochirí manuscript, written in Quechua, *Dioses y Hombres de Huarochirí* (*c*.1610), records the myths of the central highlands of Peru. Two other sources relate accounts of the mythology of the peoples of the north Peruvian coast: Cabello de Balboa's *Miscelánea Antártica* (1586) and Antonio de la Calancha's *Crónica moralizada del Orden de San Augustínen el Perú* (1638).

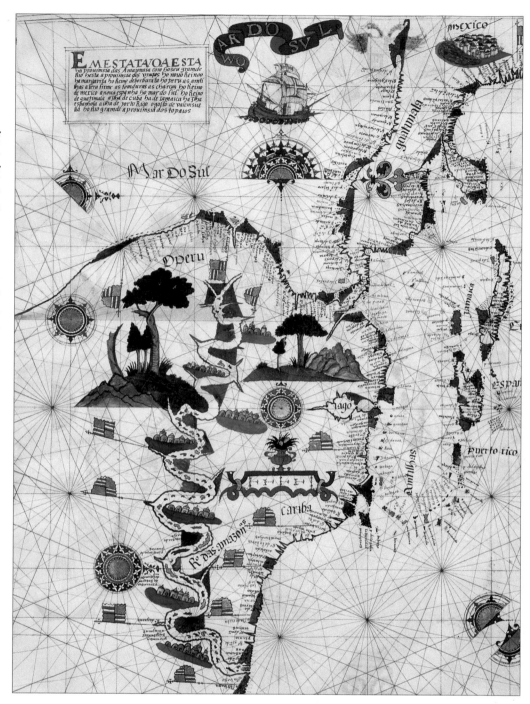

THE CHRONICLERS

Accounts of mythology written by various Spanish-trained native Quechua-speaking authors include *Nueva Crónica y Buen Gobierno* by Felipe Guaman Poma de Ayala, written between 1583 and 1613, and *Relación de Antiguedades deste Reyno del Pirú*, which was written by Juan de Santacruz Yamqui Salcamaygua about 1613. Another set of documents, known as *idolatrías*, are records by Spanish priests and investigators who were attempting to stamp out idolatrous practices known to persist among the local populace under Spanish rule. These 17th-century documents are rich

Above: An early navigational map of the Spanish possessions in the Caribbean, New Spain, northern Peru and the Amazon.

in information on local myth based on interrogations of local authorities, native curers and 'witches' and other local diviners.

Lastly, the Jesuit priest Bernabé de Cobo, drawing principally from earlier chronicles, compiled the most balanced and comprehensive synthesis of Inca history and religion, in his monumental 20-year work *Historia del Nuevo Mundo*, books 13 and 14 of which, in particular, deal with Inca religion and customs.

LANGUAGES, DRAWINGS AND *QUIPU*

Hundreds of languages and dialects were spoken by the peoples throughout the Inca Empire, a fact even enshrined in Inca creation history. However, with no written language, the Incas relied on fine-line engraving and knot tying to keep records. Both these methods of recording data, events and customs provide modern scholars with valuable information with which to interpret the artefacts and structures from archaeological excavations. A combination of these finds and the information provided by the fine-line drawing and *quipus* enables us to discern the vast workings of the Inca Empire, and even pre-Inca times, and gives a greater understanding of Inca and other Andean cultures' beliefs about the universe.

Above: An Early Intermediate Period Moche pot with a 'narrative' scene, here showing weavers using backstrap looms.

QUECHUA, AYMARA, MOCHICA

The principal language of the Incas was Quechua (known to them as *Runa Simi*). This language was used throughout the empire for its administration and economic functions. Aymará, generally thought by linguists to be older than Quechua, was spoken throughout the highland region around the basin of Lake Titicaca. Some scholars group the two languages together under the name Quechuamaran. In northern coastal Peru, Mochica was spoken, the language of the ancient Moche, their ancestors and descendants. Both Quechua and Aymará are widely spoken today in the Central Andes by some six million or more people. Mochica continued to be spoken in part of northern coastal Peru up to the beginning of the 20th century.

FINE-LINES IMAGES

Neither the Incas nor any of their Andean ancestors invented writing, and there are therefore no native historical records. However, fine-line drawings on pots reveal a great deal.

The graphic scenes they show provide records of a sort, depicting events. While such scenes are not specific historical events, many Moche fine-line drawings on ceramic vessels depict images representing commonly occurring episodes or practices in the culture. Such depictions provide invaluable information that contributes to the understanding of finds from archaeological excavations. For example, fine-line scenes of figures in burial rituals show deities, or priests-shamans in the roles of deities, which explains the presence of masks on the faces of the dead in Moche elite burials.

RECORDING WITH KNOTS

The *quipu* (or *khipu*; Quechua for 'knot') was a unique Inca Andean recording device. It comprised a central cord to which were attached numerous subsidiary cords or strings, like a fringe. The subsidiary cords were of different colours and they were tied into different sorts of knots with differing meanings. *Quipus* were mostly made of cotton cord, but llama wool was also sometimes used. About 700 *quipus* have been found.

ACCOUNTS OF MANY COLOURS

According to 16th- and 17th-century sources, prominent among which are the 16th-century conquistador and governor of Cuzco, Garcilaso de la Vega's *Comentarios Reales de los Incas* and the 17th-century *Historia et Rudimenta Linguae Piruanorum*, *quipus* had several uses.

Below: An Inca quipucamayoq *depicted by Guaman Poma de Ayala in his* Nueva Crónica y Buen Gobierno, c.1613.

Right: An Inca quipu, *which is unusually attached to a wooden rod. Specific* quipus *held records for individual cities.*

They were account 'books', in which the different colours, knots and sequences served as tallies of goods in Inca storehouses throughout the empire, or censuses of labour groups and sources; and they were mnemonic aids for recalling oral traditions – historical-literary events, including what modern scholars would call myth and legend.

The Incas used the decimal system in counting and knew positional mathematics. Knots in different positions on the same string and different types of knot were used to record thousands, hundreds and single units. The Incas were also aware of the concept of zero, duly represented by a cord without any knots. The key to reading such numerical *quipu* knots and positions was discovered in 1912 by Leland L. Locke. Analysing a *quipu* in the American Museum of Natural History, New York, he compared its knots and their positions to descriptions by Garcilaso de la Vega.

Additional meaning was recorded in the *quipu* through the use of colours and their sequences and combinations. Colours used included white, blue, yellow, red, black, green, grey, light brown and dark brown. Colours and their combinations represented types of goods or produce. For example, yellow could represent gold or maize corn.

SUBTLETIES OF MEANING

Further sophistication in meaning is represented by the orders of strings in series of the same colour. For example, in a counting of weapons stores, the most important ('noble') weapon was recorded at the left, and less noble weapons, in descending order, towards the right. The direction of the twisting of a cord itself added another layer of meaning: cords twisted to 'S' (clockwise) meant that the entire group referred to male categories

or subject matter, while cords twisted to 'Z' (anti-clockwise) meant that the entire group referred to female categories or subject matter. Even individual knots can be made clockwise or anti-clockwise.

So-called 'literary' *quipus* incorporated textile ideograms (symbols used to represent whole words or concepts) among the strings. The same ideograms are found on Inca and pre-Inca textiles, pottery, sculpture and metalwork. The positions and numbers of knots below the ideograms indicate the syllables to be 'read'. The ideograms themselves relate to Inca (Andean) concepts of the universe, and to deities, man, animals and holy objects. An ideogram can also refer to a concept such as creation, the beginning of something, or to the elements and directions as represented by colours.

NAMING PLACES

The most recent breakthrough in *quipu* analysis has been made by Gary Urton and Carrie Brezine of Harvard University. Using a computer program designed to analyse the knot patterns in 21 *quipus* from a site in Puruchuco, an Inca administrative centre on the Peruvian coast, they discovered a recurring sequence of three figure-of-eight knots that appeared to represent a place name. The placement of this sequence at the start of these *quipus* represents the name for Puruchuco, and the patterns of colour combinations and string lengths appear to rank three levels of authority among them. Thus, wherever these *quipus* went, they could be identified with the Puruchuco administration and with Inca hierarchy, passing instructions down from high-level officials.

EXPLORERS AND ARCHAEOLOGISTS

The Spanish conquistadors peppered their chronicles with descriptions that gave glimpses of the Inca way of life. The accounts and histories of colonial officials and priests attempted to provide a complete record of Inca history, society and religion, even if biased consciously or unconsciously. In the 18th and 19th centuries, these publications began to be re-examined by European and American scholars. Excavations, crude for the most part, had begun to be undertaken in Europe and America by antiquarians curious to understand their own and other's pasts and eager to make collections of antiquities for museums.

TRAVELLERS' TALES

Although most such early 'archaeological' activity in the Americas took place in North America, some scholars and travellers began to realize that there were also

Below: Alexander von Humboldt travelled throughout South America gathering information for his treatise on the continent.

Above: Alexander von Humboldt made the first attempts to collect Inca and pre-Inca antiquities and to understand their sequence.

ruins and remnants of ancient structures and artefacts throughout what had been the Inca Empire and elsewhere in South America. Paramount among these was Alexander von Humboldt (1769–1859).

Von Humboldt was the epitome of the late 18th/early 19th-century natural historian. As a gentleman traveller, scholar and popular lecturer, his travels were a combination of exploration, adventure and a pursuit of new knowledge, as he sought to uncover the continent's natural history, geography, geology and ancient history. In his two landmark publications – *Political Essay on the Kingdom of New Spain* (1811) and *Researches Concerning the Institutions and Monuments of the Ancient Inhabitants of America* (1814) – and in popular lectures he attempted to accumulate and record systematically as much data about the Americas as he could and to present it in a detailed but succinct manner. He attempted to remain unbiased in the way he recorded the data, trying to keep recorded fact and description separate from interpretation and speculation. Nevertheless, he was at

Right: Alphons Stübel at the Gateway of the Sun, Middle Horizon Tiwanaku. He published his notes with Max Uhle in 1892.

the same time a pioneer in his attempts to explain the presence of humans in the New World and their manner of coming and spreading throughout the two continents, as well as the apparent independent rise of sophisticated civilizations whose ruins were plain to see. His work and lectures brought international recognition to the antiquities of South America.

Following von Humboldt's example, and no doubt inspired by the explorations of John L. Stephens and Frederick Catherwood in Mesoamerica, books listing and describing sites and types of artefacts were published from the 1850s, and attempts were made to establish a historical framework for the bewildering amount of material that was being rediscovered about the ancient ruins of Peru and Bolivia especially. Frances de Castelnau published his *Expédition dans les Parties Centrales de l'Amérique du Sud, Troisuème Partie: Antiquités des Incas et Autre peuples Anciens* in 1854; Johann Tschudi his

Below: Ceramic kero *drinking vessels such as these were brought to private collectors and museums in the 18th and 19th centuries.*

five-volume *Reisen durch Süd Amerika* in 1869; Charles Wiener his *Pérou et Bolivie* in 1874; Ephraim G. Squier, echoing Stephens and Catherwood, his *Peru: Incidents of Travel and Exploration in the Land of the Incas* in 1877; and E. W. Middendorf his three-volume *Peru* in 1893–5, all primarily descriptive works.

DESCRIPTION AND EXCAVATION

Books and papers by Sir Clements Markham in 1856–1910, especially *A History of Peru* (1892) and *The Incas of Peru* (1910), were early attempts to synthesize and explain the data. A few scholars went one step further and actually undertook excavations: Alphons Stübel and Wilhelm Reiss excavated the Ancon cemetery on the Peruvian coast, an ancient burial place near Lima, and published their results in *The Necropolis of Ancón in Peru* (1880–7). Adolph Bandelier carried out excavations of Tiwanaku sites on Islands in the Titicaca Basin, the results of which were published in 1910, and of Tiwanaku itself in 1911.

Bridging the development of archaeology between these early classifications and descriptions of Andean materials stands the all-important figure of Max Uhle (1856–1944), who was inspired by Alphons Stübel. In 1892 he collaborated with him to publish *Die Ruinenstaette von Tiahuanaco*, a study based on notes and photographs taken by Stübel at Tiwanaku. From 1892 to 1912, Uhle carried out

regular fieldwork in Peru and Bolivia. Armed with a thorough knowledge of Inca and Tiwanaku pottery types, his excavations at Pachacamac on the Peruvian coast enabled him to establish the first breakthrough in the modern construction of the chronology of Andean ancient history. He knew Inca pottery to be 15th and 16th century in date; likewise he knew that Tiwanaku pottery was pre-Inca and completely unlike Inca ceramics. Therefore, he reasoned that the pottery he excavated at Pachacamac, because it was unlike Tiwanaku ware but was sometimes associated in layers with Inca ceramics at Pachacamac, must come between the two in date.

Uhle's work was the beginning of the assessment of series of styles of artefacts in combination with their relative position in the earth to build a chronology of the ancient cultures of the Andes. During the next 30 years he carried out other excavations, including work in Ecuador and northern Chile. He synthesized his own and others' work into a Peruvian area-wide chronology, the first for the Andean region, because he also linked his Ecuadorian and Chilean finds to the sequence. While many other scholars – European, North American and South American – worked throughout South America into the early 20th century, most of their work was limited to collecting, describing and classifying museum pieces.

MODERN INVESTIGATIONS

Modern methods in archaeology began in the 20th century. Alongside increasingly sophisticated reasoning to establish chronological sequences and relationships among artefacts and site structures, more careful methods of excavation and recording and numerous new scientific methods brought greater understanding – but also more questions. Archaeologists were no longer content just to describe, classify, date and display the past: they wanted to interpret and explain it too.

SEEKING ANSWERS TO QUESTIONS

Recording of stratigraphy (distinctive earth layers or associations between architectural features) enabled archaeologists to understand and interpret the relationships between artefacts, structures and other features. Archaeologists throughout the Americas began to direct their fieldwork towards finding evidence to answer special questions and understanding a much wider and deeper picture of ancient history. Investigations

Below: Late 20th-century excavations near the Coricancha in modern Cuzco revealed Inca foundations and water channels.

Above: The Black and White Portal at the Early Horizon temple at Chavín de Huántar. Early 20th-century archaeologists realized this was one of the first pre-Inca civilizations.

sought evidence on all aspects and classes of ancient society, not just on the elite and the exquisite.

In addition to excavations at the ruins of individual ancient cities, area surveys began to establish the extent of ancient remains, the relationships between them and the varying importance of different regions. Work focused on specific questions and historical problems: When did people first arrive in the Andes?

When was the first pottery made? When did agriculture begin? How great was the influence of different cultures, kingdoms and empires?

Excavations yielded increasing amounts of metalwork and textiles and evidence of the artefacts and methods used to make them. Studies went beyond describing and classifying the art on ancient Andean pottery and stonework and explained the meaning of their depiction of scenes and religious events.

MAKING DATES

During the first 60 years of the 20th century, Alfred L. Kroeber and John H. Rowe refined and expanded the timescale of Andean prehistory. On the basis of which materials were found and where they lay within the site's stratigraphy, Rowe defined a 'master sequence' of alternating Periods and Horizons that broadly defined the course of Andean ancient history. In the late 1940s the discovery of radiocarbon dating began to provide absolute dates for these cultural periods.

The first native Peruvian archaeologist, Julio C. Tello, began a life-long career excavating sites of the earliest periods of Andean civilization, notably Paracas cemetery on Peru's southern coast, Sechín Alto in northern Peru and Chavín de Huántar in the central Andes. He defined these remote periods when Andean civilization began and distinctive socio-economic and religious traits were established. In 1939, Tello and Kroeber established the Institute of Andean Research. Similarly, Luis E. Valcarcel, Tello's successor at the Lima Museo Nacional, promoted the rich interchange between different fields of study to clarify Inca and pre-Inca society.

INTERNATIONAL EXPEDITIONS

After World War Two, large-scale, long-running projects were undertaken throughout the Andes, addressing every period, from the earliest inhabitants to the Incas. Principal among these was the Virú Valley Project, begun in 1946 by Wendell C. Bennett, William D. Strong, James A. Ford, Clifford Evans, Gordon R. Willey, Junius Bird and Donald Collier.

In the 1960s and 1970s, Edward Lanning, Thomas Patterson and Michael Moseley worked on the central Peruvian coast. Thomas Lynch, Richard MacNeish and others clarified the Palaeoindian period. Seiichi Izumi and Toshihiko Sono of Tokyo University investigated Kotosh and

other early ceramic ceremonial sites. Luis G. Lumbreras and Hernán Amat renewed the study of Chavín de Huántar, as did Richard L. Burger of the Peabody Museum. Donald Lathrap and his students worked in the eastern Andes and adjacent lowlands.

In the 1960s to 1980s, John Rowe, John Murra, Tom Zuidema, Gary Urton and many others renewed the study of the Incas, including excavations at Huánuco Pampa by Craig Morris and Donald Thompson. Large-scale projects were undertaken by Michael Moseley and Carol Mackay at Chan Chan, by William Isbell at Huari, by Christopher Donnan and Izumi Shimada in the Moche Valley and by Alan Kolata in the Tiwanaku Basin.

No summary of 20th-century Andean archaeology can ignore three of its most spectacular discoveries. In 1911 the young explorer Hiram Bingham rediscovered the Inca fortress and ceremonial precinct of Machu Picchu in the remote Urubamba Valley north of Cuzco, bringing it to world fame. In the 1980s, Walter Alva and Susana Meneses made astounding discoveries and excavations of fabulous, unlooted elite Moche tombs at Sipán in the Lambeyeque Valley of northern Peru. And in 1995 Johan Reinhard and Miguel Zárate discovered rich child

Left: John H. Rowe recording findings at the Inca palace of Huyna Capac, at Quisphuanca, Peru.

Above: Late 20th-century excavations by Walter Alva of the rare unlooted tomb of an Early Intermediate Period Moche lord at Sipán in the Lambayeque Valley, Peru.

burials high on Mt Ampato in the southern Andes, explaining the Inca ritual of *capacocha* sacrifice.

RETURN TO SOURCES

Alongside 20th- and 21st-century excavations and analyses, archaeologists still return to the original texts: the chronicles and records of the conquistadors and colonial officials. However biased or conflicting these may sometimes be, they remain the only first-hand accounts of Inca society. Uhle knew that the ruins of Tiwanaku were pre-Inca because the Incas themselves told the Spaniards that the city lay in ruins when they subjugated the area. Similarly, when Morris and Thompson discovered 497 stone structures arranged in orderly rows along the hillside south of Huánuco Pamapa, the stacked pottery vessels of agricultural produce revealed these buildings to be none other than examples of Inca provincial storehouses in which, as described in the chronicles, they collected the wealth of the empire for redistribution.

In this way, the first Spanish accounts continue to help explain excavation finds and to provide a basis for interpreting aspects of pre-Inca civilization, whose material remains often demonstrate a link with Inca practices and social functions.

PART ONE

HISTORY

The vast continent of South America may form a more or less separate physical unit, but the ancient peoples who once lived there never formed a single culture. For this reason we cannot assess the continent as a whole but need to describe the people, culture, religion and mythology of each of many different groups.

Urban-based societies were confined to the Andes Mountains and nearby western coastal valleys and deserts. Cultures that built ceremonial centres, governed large areas and developed advanced metalwork, pottery, textiles and stone-carving technologies in present-day western Venezuela, Colombia, Peru, Bolivia, northern Chile and northwestern Argentina. In this book, this area is defined as the 'Andean Area'. Peoples elsewhere in South America developed sophisticated societies with complex religious beliefs, but they did not build monumental ceremonial centres or cities, develop technology of quite the same complexity or build kingdoms and empires.

The nature of the landscape itself provided stimuli for civilized societies to develop. Within a relatively small area the land ranges from Pacific coastal plains and deserts, with coastal valleys ascending east into the Andean foothills, to high mountain valleys and plateaux, then to the eastern Andean slopes descending to the high pampas and rainforests. A key factor in the development and endurance of these civilizations was water, which was important functionally as well as symbolically and religiously.

The administrative centre of Huanuco Pampa contained rows of great warehouses built of finely carved blocks of stone fitted together without mortar.

TIMELINE: THE INCAS AND THEIR ANCESTORS

CHRONOLOGY OF ANDEAN AREA CIVILIZATION

The chronology of the Andean Area is complex. Archaeologists have developed a scheme based on technological achievements and on changing political organization through time, from the first arrival of humans in the area (15,000–3500BC) to the conquest of the Inca Empire by Francisco Pizarro in 1532. The pace of technological development varied in different regions within the Andean Area, especially during early periods in its history. The development of lasting and strong contact between regions, however,

Below: A wooden cup painted with an Inca warrior with shield and axe-spear.

spread both technology and ideas, and led to regions depending on each other to some degree. Sometimes this interdependence was due to large areas being under the control of one 'authority', while at other times the unifying link was religious or based on trade and technology.

The principal chronological scheme for the Andean Area comprises a sequence of eight time units: five Periods and three Horizons. Periods are defined as times when political unity across regions was less consolidated. Smaller areas were controlled by city-states, sometimes in loose groupings, perhaps sharing religious beliefs despite having different political organizations. The Horizons, by contrast, were times when much larger political units were formed. These units exercised political, economic and religious control over extended areas, usually including different types of terrain, rather than being confined to coastal valley groups or sierra city-states.

Different scholars give various dates for the beginnings and endings of the Periods and Horizons, and no two books on Andean civilization give exactly the same dates. The durations of Periods and

Above: The sacred Intihuatana (Hitching Post of the Sun) at Machu Picchu.

Horizons also vary from one region to another within the Andean Area, and charts increase in complexity as authors divide the Andean Area into coastal, sierra and Altiplano regions, or even into north, central and southern coastal regions and north, central and southern highland regions. The dates given here are a compilation from several sources, thus avoiding any anomalies among specific sources.

CHRONOLOGICAL PERIOD	DATES	PRINCIPAL CULTURES
Lithic / Archaic Period	15,000–3500BC	spread of peoples into the Andean Area hunter-gatherer cultures
Preceramic / Formative Period (Cotton Preceramic)	3500–1800BC	early agriculture and first ceremonial centres
Initial Period	1800–750BC	U-shaped ceremonial centres, platform mounds and sunken courts
Early Horizon	750–200BC	Chavín, Paracas, Pukará (Yaya-Mama) cults
Early Intermediate Period	200BC–AD600	Moche, Nazca and Titicaca Basin confederacies
Middle Horizon	AD600–1000	Wari and Tiwanaku empires
Late Intermediate Period	AD1000–1400	Chimú and Inca empires
Late Horizon	AD1400–1532	Inca Empire and Spanish Conquest

LITHIC / ARCHAIC PERIOD (40,000–3500BC)

Above: This mummified body from the Chinchorros culture is 8,000 years old.

*c.*40,000 to *c.*20,000 years ago Ice-free corridors open up across the Bering Strait, but there is no evidence humans entered the New World until the late stages of this time period.

*c.*20,000BC Migrating hunter-gatherers, using stone-, bone-, wood- and shell-tool technologies, probably enter the New World from north-east Asia.

from *c.*15,000 years ago Palaeoindians migrate south and east to populate the Americas, reaching Monte Verde in southern Chile *c.*14,850 years ago.

*c.*8500–5000BC Hunter-gatherers occupy cave and rock shelter sites in the Andes (e.g. Pachamachay, Guitarrero, Tres Ventana and Toquepala caves). Evidence of tending of hemp-like fibre, medicinal plants, herbs and wild tubers.

*c.*5000BC First mummified burials in the Atacama Desert, Chinchorros culture.

Below: Mountains high in the Andes proved a challenge to early settlers.

PRECERAMIC / FORMATIVE PERIOD (3500–1800BC)

Above: Preceramic Period sculpture at the Temple of the Crossed Hands, Kotosh.

This period is sometimes also called the Cotton Preceramic.

*c.*3500–1800BC True plant domestication accomplished – cotton, squashes and gourds, beans, maize, potatoes, sweet potatoes, beans, chilli peppers. Llamas and other camelids herded on the Altiplano.

*c.*3000BC Coastal fishing villages such as Huaca Prieta flourish, using gourd containers but no ceramics, and produce early cotton textiles.

*c.*2800BC Early northern coastal civic-ceremonial centres begin at Aspero – Huaca de los Idolos and Huaca de los Sacrificios.

*c.*2400–2000BC Large, raised mound platforms are constructed at El Paraíso, La Galagada and Kotosh – Temple of the Crossed Hands. Spread of the Kotosh religious cult.

Below: Llamas and other camelids were first domesticated during this period.

INITIAL PERIOD (1800–750BC)

Above: View of the Colca Canyon shows terracing that began in this period.

Spread of pottery, irrigation agriculture, monumental architecture; religious processions and ritual decapitation begin.

from *c.*1800BC Sophisticated irrigation systems develop in coastal oases valleys, the highlands and Altiplano.

*c.*1800BC Construction at Moxeke includes colossal adobe heads.

*c.*1750BC Builders at La Florida bring the first pottery to this region.

*c.*1500BC Cerro Sechín flourishes.

*c.*1400–1200BC Sechín Alto becomes the largest U-shaped civic-ceremonial centre in the New World.

*c.*1300BC Construction of the five platform mounds at Cardál.

*c.*900BC U-shaped ceremonial complex at Chavín de Huántar begins.

Below: Garagay, central Peru, was a typical coastal U-shaped civic-ceremonial centre.

EARLY HORIZON (750–200BC)

Above: A stone severed head, with feline canines, from Chavín de Huántar.

Religious cults develop around Chavín de Huántar and Pukará. Decapitation, hallucinogenic drug use, spiritual transformation and ancestor worship become widespread.

from *c.*750BC The Old Temple at Chavín becomes established as a cult centre. Influence of the Lanzón deity and the Staff Deity spreads. The Paracas Peninsula serves as the necropolis site for several settlements, and the Oculate Being is shown on textiles and ceramics.

*c.*400–200BC The Old Temple at Chavín is enlarged to create the New Temple. The Chavín Cult spreads, especially at Kuntur Wasi and Karwa (Paracas).

*c.*400BC Rainfall fell in the Titicaca Basin. Pukará, northwest of the lake, is established, and becomes the centre of the Yaya-Mama cult.

*c.*200BC Chavín Cult influence waned.

Below: Vicuñas at Viscachani, now in Bolivia, were prized for their fine wool.

EARLY INTERMEDIATE PERIOD (200BC–AD600)

Above: The closely set stone blocks of the external walls of Sacsahuaman, Cusco.

The cohesion of Chavín disintegrates, and several regional chiefdoms develop in the coastal and mountain valleys.

from *c.*100BC Rise of the Nazca .

*c.*AD100 Burial of the Old Lord of Sipán in Lambayeque Valley.

*c.*AD100 to 500 The Nazca sacred ceremonial centre of Cahuachi flourishes.

*c.*1st century AD The Moche dynasty is founded in the northern coastal valleys.

*c.*AD250 Rise of oracle of Pachacamac.

*c.*AD300 Burial of the Lord of Sipán in Lambayeque Valley.

*c.*AD500 The Moche ceremonial platforms of the Huacas del Sol and de la Luna are the largest in the area.

*c.*AD700 Moche/Nazca power wanes.

Below: This giant Nazca desert geoglyph of the spider is visible from space.

MIDDLE HORIZON (AD600–1000)

Above: The Staff Deity depicted on the Gateway of the Sun at Tiwanaku.

Much of the Andean Area is unified in two empires: Tiwanaku in the south and Wari in the north. They share common beliefs around the creator god Viracocha.

*c.*AD300 Major construction of the central ceremonial plaza at Tiwanaku begins.

*c.*AD400–750 Major phases of building of elite residential quarters at Tiwanaku.

*c.*AD500 The rise of Huari, capital of the Wari Empire.

by *c.*AD600 Huari is a flourishing capital city and rival to Tiwanaku.

*c.*AD650 Pikillacta, the southernmost Wari city, is founded.

*c.*AD750–1000 Third major phase of palace building at Tiwanaku.

*c.*AD900–950 Burial of the Sicán Lords at Lambayeque.

Below: The reed boats on Lake Titicaca have been made for thousands of years.

LATE INTERMEDIATE PERIOD
(AD1000–1400)

Above: The Late Intermediate Period Sicán Tucume pyramid, Lambayeque Valley.

An era of political break up is characterized by new city-states, including Lambayeque, Chimú and Pachacamac, the Colla and Lupaka kingdoms, and numerous city-states in the central and southern Andean valleys.

*c.*AD1000 Tiwannaku and Wari empires wane as regional political rivalry reasserts itself.

*c.*AD1000 Wari city-state is abandoned.

*c.*AD1000 Chan Chan, the Chimú capital, is founded in the Moche valley.

*c.*1100 The Incas under Manco Capac, migrate into the Cuzco Valley, found Cuzco and establish the Inca dynasty.

*c.*1250 City of Tiwanaku abandoned, perhaps because of changes in climate.

*c.*1300 Sinchi Roca becomes the first emperor to use the title Sapa Inca.

Below: The city of Cuzco was founded by Manco Capac, its legendary first ruler.

LATE HORIZON
(AD1400–1532)

Above: The Inca hillside site of Winay Wayna overlooks the Urubamba River.

In just over 130 years the Incas build a huge empire and establish an imperial cult centred on Inti, the sun god, whose representative on earth is the Sapa Inca.

*c.*1425 Viracocha begins the Inca conquest of the Cuzco Valley.

1438 Pachacuti Inca Yupanqui defeats the Chancas to dominate the Cuzco Valley.

1438–71 Pachacuti begins the rebuilding of Cuzco as the imperial capital to the plan of a crouching puma.

1471 Fall of the Kingdom of Chimú.

1471–93 Inca Tupac Yupanqui expands the empire west and south, doubling its size.

1493–1526 Huayna Capac consolidates the empire, building fortresses, road systems, storage redistribution and religious precincts throughout the provinces.

Below. The Spaniards built S Domingo on the foundations of the Inca Coricancha.

Above: Manco Capac, legendary founder of the Inca dynasty and 'son of the sun'.

1526 Huayna Capac dies of smallpox without an agreed successor.

1526–32 Huayna Capac's son Huáscar seizes the throne but is challenged by his brother Atahualpa. A six-year civil war ends in the capture of Huáscar.

1530 Inca Empire at its greatest extent.

1532 Francisco Pizarro lands with a small army on the north coast and marches to meet Atahualpa at Cajamarca.

1532 Battle of Cajamarca and capture of Atahualpa, who is held for ransom.

1533 Atahualpa is executed.

1535 Francisco Pizarro founds Lima as his capital in Spanish Peru.

1541 Pizarro assassinated in his palace at Lima by Almagro and his associates.

Below: The sacred site of Machu Picchu was rediscovered by Hiram Bingham in 1911.

CHAPTER ONE

EMPIRE OF THE SUN

The Incas were a small group, or tribe, numbering perhaps 40,000 individuals or fewer in the Huantanay (Cuzco) Valley of modern central Peru. They were one group among many in the valley. Through conquest, first locally then beyond the valley, they built the largest empire that ever existed in the Americas. At its greatest extent, in AD1530, its northern border coincided roughly with the modern Ecuadorian–Colombian border, its southern extent stretched to modern central Chile, to the east it claimed regions into the lowlands bordering the Amazon Rainforest, and to the west it met the Pacific Ocean. Yet the Incas' rise to power lasted less than 100 years, and during the whole of this time they were engaged in wars of conquest or in the civil war at the end of this period.

Pachacuti Inca Yupanqui founded the imperial state of the Incas, and under his rule the Incas continued to dominate the Cuzco Valley. As the empire expanded, vast networks of roads were built to unite its far corners, coupled with impressive architectural and engineering feats that enabled planned towns and cities with great monuments to be built. Bridges were built and existing systems of terracing and irrigation expanded.

When the Spaniards under the leadership of Francisco Pizarro first arrived, the empire was still being expanded, but by the time of their third visit the empire was split by civil war. This war led eventually to the death of two rival sons of the Inca ruler, Huayna Capac, and the victory of Pizarro.

Left: The skilled metallurgists of the La Tolita culture were among many to depict the sun as a rayed golden mask.

LAND OF THE FOUR QUARTERS

The Incas called their world Tahuantin-suyu (or Tawantinsyu), literally meaning 'the land of the four united quarters'. Cuzco, the capital city, formed the focal point (although it was not the geographical centre) on which the four quarters were oriented and from which they emanated.

To the north-east of Cuzco was Antisuyu, the smallest quarter and the only one that did not border on the Pacific Ocean. To the north-west, stretching to the northernmost borders of the empire, was Chinchaysuyu. This quarter's northern extent had, in fact, only recently been extended into Quito province by the last conquering Sapa Inca, Huayna Capac (1493–1526), shortly before the arrival of the conquistador Francisco Pizarro in 1531. South and west of Cuzco was Cuntisuyu, second in size, and to the south-east was the largest of the four quarters, Collasuyu.

Below: Ephraim George Squier was the first to show a detailed plan of Inca Cuzco as a puma, its head formed by the fortress-temple of Sacsahuaman and its body and tail by the streets and water channels.

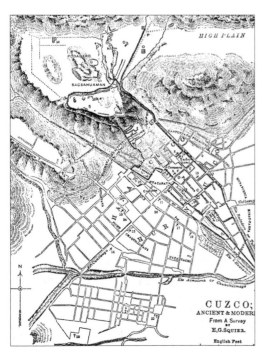

Above: The Huacaypata Plaza, Cuzco, now the Plaza de Armas, was the site of ritual celebrations at solstices and festivals.

UNEQUAL QUARTERS

The four quarters were not only unequal in size but in population. They also differed extensively in the types of terrain they encompassed. Together they comprised a vast territory stretching from modern Ecuador to central Chile, north to south, and from the Pacific coast to the eastern flank of the Andes mountain chain, west to east. The empire was inhabited by a great variety of peoples and languages, each with long traditions of local devel-opment, masterfully united and socially co-ordinated and manipulated by their Inca masters. The Incas recognized this diversity as the deliberate actions of the creator god Viracocha, who, having formed the second world and its human inhabitants out of clay, dispersed them after giving them the clothing, skills and languages of the different tribes and nations.

Mention of the partition of the empire into four quarters was, as such, virtually ignored in most of Inca history. One legend, however, recounted in Garcilaso de la Vega's early 17th-century work, *Commentarios Reales de los Incas*, describes the division as the work of an 'Un-named

Man' who appeared at Tiwanaku after the destruction of a previous world by great floods. This near lack of explanation is especially curious given the emphasis in Inca legendary history on the progress of the state creation from Lake Titicaca – near the geographical centre of the empire – towards the north and west, into the Huantanay (Cuzco) Valley.

This progress in one direction makes sense for Antisuyu, Chinchaysuyu and Cuntisuyu, but not for Collasuyu, which lies almost entirely to the south of Lake Titicaca. One explanation might lie in the fact that the Incas recast the origin mythology of the peoples of Collasuyu in order to bolster their own claims of origin from the Titicaca Basin, thus legit-imizing their right to rule the region. The Incas were aware of the remains of Tiwanaku to the south and west of the lake, and no doubt of the relics of other previous great cities of the region, and must have recognized them as the centres

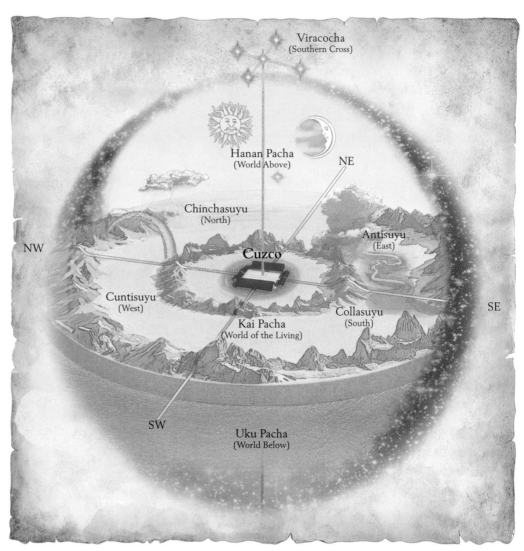

Right: A diagram of the land of the four quarters, based on a 1613 sketch by Juan de Santa Cruz Pachacuti Ymaqui Salcamaygua.

of former power bases. The Incas explained to the Spaniards that Tiwanaku lay in ruins when they invaded and conquered the Titicaca Basin.

THE FOUNDING OF CUZCO

The Incas regarded their capital at Cuzco as being at the centre of the world. Once again, Inca legendary history and heavenly associations formed the basis of their arrangments, for Cuzco equally reflected state and celestial organization. According to legend, Pachacuti Inca rebuilt the imperial city and the Coricancha (Sun Temple) in stone, being inspired by the ruined stone masonry of Tiwanaku. Indeed, archaeological excavations in the capital have shown that the Incas had no tradition of megalithic stone masonry before about AD1350–75, according to radiocarbon dating. The city was divided into upper (*hanan*) and lower (*hurin*) sections, respectively the quarters of the two social divisions of the populace believed to have been ordered by the first ruler, Manco Capac. Again according to legend,

Left: Inca surveyors linked the provinces of the entire empire with a masterly engineered road system.

Pachacuti named the renewed city 'lion's body' (by which the Spanish chronicler meant a puma), and, from above, the plan of the city indeed resembles a crouching puma with a head and tail.

,

HIGHWAYS AND LINES

From the central plaza, Huacaypata, four great imperial highways and four sacred cosmic lines radiated to the four quarters. From the nearby Coricancha emanated 41 sacred *ceque* lines: sightings lines to the horizons and beyond. They were grouped into upper and lower sets and further divided into four quarters. The upper set was associated with Hanan Cuzco and with the quarters of Antisuyu (north-east) and Chinchasuyu (north-west), while the lower set was associated with Hurin Cuzco and with the quarters of Collasuyu (south-east) and Cuntisuyu

(south-west). Together these highways, cosmic lines and *ceques* integrated the capital and the four quarters into the Inca state religion focused on Inti, the sun god, as a near equal to the creator Viracocha – perhaps another reason why they did not emphasize the history of the divisions.

ROADMAP OF THE STARS

A link with the heavens was further enhanced by the association of each of the four great highways along a route approximating (except when having to to go around hills and mountains) a north–south/east–west axis of Mayu (literally 'celestial river'), commonly known as the Milky Way. In the course of 24 hours, ancient Andeans observed that Mayu crosses its zenith in the sky, and in so doing forms two intersecting axes oriented north-east/south-west and south-east/north-west. Thus, the divisions of the sky provided a celestial grid against which their world of Tahuantinsuyu was projected.

CUZCO AND BEYOND

The Inca Empire stretched more than 4,200km (2,600 miles) from north to south and east to west across the Andes, from the Amazon rainforests and Argentine plains to the Pacific coast. Throughout this vast area lived a variety of peoples whose earlier cultural evolution united them locally and regionally, especially at an economic and religious level. This was exploited by the Incas, who imposed imperial rule and economic stability on the empire.

ALL ROADS LEAD TO CUZCO

Imperial Cuzco, the capital city, was considered to be the navel of the Inca world. From it and to it led all roads, both physically and spiritually. This network linked peoples and cultures as varied as fishing communities, such as the Uru in the Lake Titicaca Basin, and the Kingdom of Chimú on the Peruvian north coast, a state whose sophistication might have rivalled the Incas. The empire reached its greatest extent beyond the Cuzco Valley in less than 100 years of conquests.

Below: Tambo Colorado, at the end of a major road running west, was one of many planned provincial administrative capitals.

SPREADING CIVILIZATION

A number of distinctive Inca cultural traits have been identified, which they spread to greater and lesser extents throughout the empire. These include: a corporate style of architecture, settlement planning, artefact styles, large-scale engineering works and terracing.

In the Cuzco area, most residential buildings (*kanchas*) were rectangular, single-room and single-storey affairs, arranged around courtyards. They were made of fieldstones or adobe bricks,

Above: The vast Altiplano of Collasuyu, Bolivia, south of Cuzco, was added to the empire through the conquests of Sapa Inca Tupac Yupanqui (1471–93).

gabled, with thatched roofs, and had doors, windows and internal niches usually of trapezoidal shape. A second basic form, the *kalanka*, was a rectangular hall used for several public functions. Structures for state purposes were mostly, but not always, made of finely cut and fitted stone. Most were in the capital and its immediate environs; fitted-stone architecture was rare in the provinces and restricted to special state buildings.

In settlement planning, the Incas practised a policy of relocating peoples away from their homelands for political and economic reasons. In such settlements, Inca engineers laid out *kancha* enclosures in blocks around Inca-style state administrative buildings where needed. Some provincial Inca settlements were established for specific purposes, perhaps one of the best known being Huánuco Pampa, an Inca imperial city about 675km (420 miles) north-west of Cuzco in the Chinchaysuyu quarter, which was established as a seat of provincial administration and also for the storage and redistribution of the products of the empire.

Above: Huánuco Pampa, a provincial administrative capital in Chinchasuyu, lay on the main northern trunk road up the spine of the empire, heading all the way to Quito.

In some provincial settlements, the Incas relied on local technology and adapted themselves to local political and social organization while retaining an over-arching control. In such cases any evidence of Inca presence, conquest and rule is found more in material culture, particularly pottery (but also textiles and metalwork), of distinctive Inca decorative design and techniques.

The vast majority of settlements were not Inca in origin and were, apart from the relocated populations in Inca-planned towns, left in their native styles and plans. Again, Huánuco Pampa provides an important example: the surrounding villages retained their local native character and Inca rule was exerted indirectly through local leaders.

Throughout the empire, Inca engineers were famous for their works. There were roads, bridges, agricultural terracing and accompanying systems of irrigation canals. Imperial highways linked Cuzco with the provincial capitals. Major imperial highways went north-west to Vilcashuaman, Huánuco Pampa, Cajamarca, Tumibamba and Quito and south-east to Chucuito, Paria, Tupiza, La Paya, Santiago and other cities. Westward-running highways branched off to major coastal cities – Tumbes, Pachacamac, Tambo Colorado, Nazca and others – and a parallel highway ran along the Peruvian coast as far as Atico. In many cases pre-existing roads were incorporated and it is often difficult to identify roads as specifically Inca-made unless there is also associated Inca architecture, or sometimes evidence of inhabitants. Similarly with bridges: it is often only the presence of stone foundations and Inca artefacts at river crossings that indicates where an Inca bridge stood.

Land terracing, especially throughout the Andes, was constructed to take advantage of every available opportunity to extend land for growing, especially maize. Again, it is not always possible to identify specifically Inca terracing from pre-Inca work without other associated Inca features, but it is certain that with the expansion of Inca domination the extent of terracing increased greatly.

KINSHIP AND TAXES

The Incas exploited and perhaps consolidated the economic and social arrangement called *ayllu*. This was a kinship charter based on actual or imagined descent between groups working the different environments between highlands and lowlands, especially farming and llama herding. Such a group of related people was an organization for both labour exchange and a common ownership of property, possessions and rights; it also established, monitored and regulated rules of social conduct, and solved social problems at various levels. In other words, it incorporated rights and responsibilities.

The Incas employed a state tax system of agricultural produce divided into three categories; land was divided accordingly to support each category. The first was for the support of the gods – in practical terms it went to the priests, other religious functionaries and shrine attendants. The second went to the emperor, to support the imperial household and into storage for redistribution in times of need. The third was for the communities themselves; it was collected, stored and distributed annually by local officials.

In addition to taxation there was a labour tax, or obligation, called *mit'a*. This was an annual draft of able-bodied males to undertake public work.

Although both *ayllu* and *mit'a* were established in pre-Inca times throughout much of the Andes, the Incas exploited and used them more extensively.

BUILDING AN EMPIRE

The Inca Empire began and ended in conflict. Its downfall was hastened by the Spanish invasion, yet, when the Spaniards arrived, the Incas were themselves engaged in civil war.

THE CUZCO VALLEY

The founding of the empire is obscured in elaborate legend and myth invented by the Incas. It began with a legendary figure and first ruler, Manco Capac, leader of the *ayars*, the legendary ancestors, and founder of the Inca dynasty. The founding involved mystical birth from the earth, the designation of Inca superiority and their destiny to rule.

There were four brothers, of whom Manco was senior, and four sisters/wives – providing consistency with the division of the empire into four quarters. It was Manco who ordered the division of the people into the *hurin* and *hanan* – the upper and the lower – and who formed 'the allies' into ten lineage groups: the ten *ayllus* of commoners at Cuzco to complement the ten royal *ayllus* of his and his brothers' descendants. After migration from Lake Titicaca and many adventures, Manco, his sister/wife, and other sisters, and their son Sinchi Roca arrived in the Valley of Cuzco, where Manco organized the building of the city. Sinchi Roca duly inherited the throne and allegedly commanded the people of the valley to cultivate potatoes. He was followed by his son Lloque Yupanqui. We have no idea how long these rulers reigned, or if there were more than are named.

Archaeology provides only hints of the development of Inca power in the Cuzco Valley. We know little of what lies buried beneath modern Cuzco, and almost nothing of what lies beneath the 16th-century Inca city. It has been occupied continuously since Inca times, if not before, and many Inca structures were themselves used as foundations for Spanish colonial and later structures.

DEVELOPING POWER

Ceramic styles show us that the Incas were probably a local tribe, one of several in the valley, and that Cuzco began to emerge as a regional centre in the Late Intermediate Period from the early 13th

Above: Manco Capac allegedly founded Inca Cuzco and ruled in the 12th century, in the Late Intermediate Period.

century. No individual buildings, or any distinctive architectural style, can be identified with the Incas or with a specific Inca ruler until the reign of Pachacuti Inca Yupanqui (1438–71). We do not know whether the Incas ruled Cuzco from this early time, coexisted with their neighbours or actually lived elsewhere.

What is certain, however, is that they began to dominate the valley from at least about the beginning of the 15th century. A sort of defined style began to emerge in the late 14th and early 15th centuries and was strengthened by Pachacuti Inca Yupanqui. It was he who began the formation of the Inca imperial state; and the Late Horizon, which began *c*.1400, is defined by the beginning of his hegemony.

The intervening rulers between Lloque Yupanqui and Pachacuti are a mere name list: Mayta Capac, Capac Yupanqui, Inca

Left: Puca Pukara fort near Cuzco was used in wars against the neighbouring peoples in the Cuzco Valley and adjacent valleys.

Roca, Yahuar Huacac, Viracocha Inca and Inca Urco. We have little knowledge of their achievements other than that they inherited rulership of the Cuzco Valley, and continued to dominate their neighbours and strengthen their power within the valley. Mayta Capac defeated a local tribe called the Alcaviçças, who were apparently dissatisfied with the Inca overlordship in the valley.

WAR AGAINST THE CHANCAS

Only Viracohca Inca and Urco emerge from legend as real people. During troubled times, undoubtedly the war with the Chancas (another valley tribe), Viracocha claimed that the god Viracocha came to him in a dream, calmed his fears and inspired him to rule. However, he and his son and named heir, Urco, fled Cuzco with much of the populace when the Chancas advanced on the city. Urco enjoyed the shortest reign – less than a year in 1438 – if he actually reigned at all.

Below: The tiered wall of Sacsahuaman, which forms the north-west quarter (Chinchasuyu) of Inca Cuzco.

His brother, Yupanqui, was more steadfast and stayed to defend the city. He too claimed divine inspiration, in an earlier incident giving him a vision of the future. In official Inca history, Yupanqui rallied his companions and repulsed the first two attacks. He called upon the gods for help and the very stones in the field allegedly became Inca warriors. The Chancas were defeated and, taking the name Pachacuti Inca ('Earth-shaker King'), he assumed the throne.

TO THE LIMITS OF THE EMPIRE

The date of 1438, which comes from the chronicler Miguel Cabello de Valboa, marked Pachacuti's defeat of the Chancas and his succession to the throne. He subdued the Cuzco Valley and declared all Quechua-speakers there to be honorary Inca citizens. He began Inca imperial aspirations by conquering the Lupaqa, Colla and other city-states to the south-east around Lake Titicaca. Then he turned his armies over to his son and chosen heir, Tupac Inca Yupanqui, to continue campaigning, while he returned to Cuzco and devoted his energies to consolidating the power of the Incas.

Above: Pachacuti Inca Yupanqui expanded the Inca Empire with conquests into Cuntisuyu, Chinchasuyu and Collasuyu.

Pachacuti is credited with developing Inca statecraft and with organizing the institutions and systems that were the hallmarks of Inca rule: national taxation and labour levies, roadways and an imperial communication network, and extensive warehousing of food and other commodities for redistribution throughout the empire. He also established the official Inca state religion based on worship of Inti – the sun – and commissioned much building in the city, including the temple-fortress of Sacsahuaman, which was dedicated to the worship of Inti.

Tupac (1471–93) extended the empire to its greatest extent with conquests to the north and south, especially of the powerful Chimú Kingdom on the north coast, defeating King Minchançaman. His successor, Huayna Capac (1493–1526), campaigned throughout the empire, largely consolidating earlier gains. He had recently subjugated the kingdom of Quito when he died suddenly of smallpox. In the turmoil that followed, two of his sons, half-brothers by different wives, claimed the succession: Huáscar, governor of Cuzco, and Atahualpa, who controlled the army in the north.

CIVIL WAR

Spanish sources leave some doubt as to whether Huayna Capac, the twelfth Inca ruler, had actually named his successor when he died suddenly. Some sources say there was an heir apparent, a young son Ninancuyuchi, others that Huayna Capac favoured his son Huáscar, or that he secretly hoped that another son, Atahualpa, would use his control of the army to supplant Huáscar. Still other sources indicate that he had planned to divide the empire among several sons, or even that the empire was so far extended that it was effectively dividing itself in 1526.

Needless to say, the various factions that still existed at the time of the Spanish conquest recited to Spanish chroniclers the versions of events and descendants that suited them. Nevertheless, upon Huayna Capac's death, the Spaniards had just arrived off the northern coast of the empire and the Incas plunged into a bloody civil war that itself threatened the demise of the empire and all it stood for.

Below: Soldiers of Atahualpa's army lead his brother Huáscar into captivity after his defeat at the Battle of Huánuco Pampa.

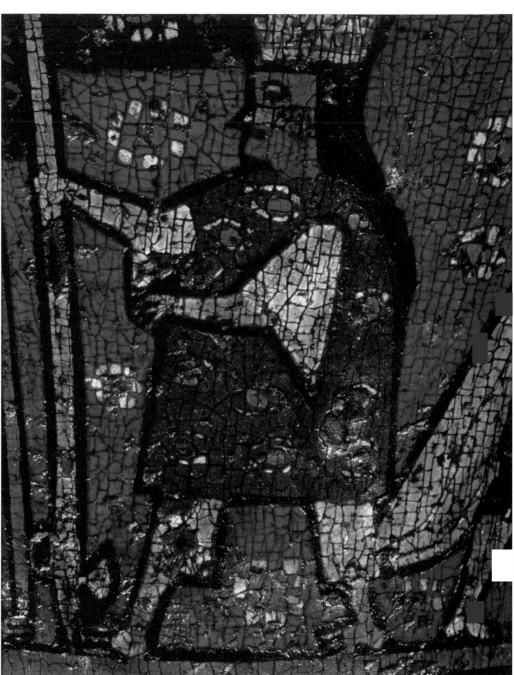

ONE THRONE: THREE HEIRS?

Huayna Capac had campaigned in the north of the empire for ten years. He had gone north, originally to quell a rebellion in Quito province, taking with him his sons Ninancuyuchi and Atahualpa. In Cuzco he left four governors, one of whom was Huáscar, another of his sons by his many wives. When an epidemic of smallpox broke out in the north and

Above: An Inca soldier painted on a wooden kero *drinking vessel, wearing traditional battle dress – a tunic and feather headdress.*

Huayna Capac contracted it, he anointed in formal ceremony his son Ninancuyuchi as his heir. But Ninancuyuchi also died of smallpox, and this situation left a dilemma and a plethora of possible claimants to the throne.

Huáscar seized the throne in Cuzco but was contested by Atahualpa, his younger half-brother. Atahualpa had been involved in the campaign against and subjugation of the Quito region in the far north of the empire. At his father's death he was left in command of the Inca armies of the north. At the death of Huayna Capac and Ninancuyuchi, he at first seemed to accept Huáscar's rise to power and ordered new palaces to be built for Huáscar in the northern city of Tumipampa. The local chief, Ullco Colla, however, resented Atahualpa and spread rumours of a plot against Huáscar. In the ensuing intrigue, Atahualpa and Huáscar became enemies and the former marched to confront his brother. The Inca court split into two supporting factions and civil war raged for six years.

BATTLE BETWEEN BROTHERS

Huáscar declared Atahualpa to be *auca* – a treasonous enemy of the state. He sent the army he commanded in Cuzco to attack Atahualpa and capture him in Quito.

Below: The imposing tiered walls of Sacsahuaman imply its use as a fortress as well as its main purpose as a temple to Inti.

But in a major battle Huáscar's forces were utterly defeated, and Atahualpa continued a relentless march south.

Huáscar sent larger armies against him. There were running battles and Huascar's forces were defeated but without conclusive results. Rivalry even broke out among Huáscar's generals. Huáscar sent even greater forces against Atahualpa, who again defeated them, until finally, in 1532, Huáscar himself marched with an army against him. Atahualpa's experience in the northern campaigns finally proved decisive, and this time Huáscar was taken prisoner. The final battle took place at Huánuco Pampa, north-west of Cuzco.

Atahualpa, whose forces were flushed with their victories, relied on speed. His generals marched immediately against Huáscar before further reinforcements could arrive from Cuzco. Given what had already transpired, Atahualpa offered no peace negotiations. The battle apparently lasted most of the day until Huáscar's troops broke and Huáscar was forced to flee with his immediate retinue of about 1,000 retainers and troops. Atahualpa's forces soon overtook him, however, seized Huáscar and put the remainder of his followers to death.

Above: Dressed in distinctive tunics and armed with axe-headed spears and shields, Inca armies subdued the empire.

ROYAL SACRILEGE

The ruthlessness of this prolonged war continued when Atahualpa marched on and captured Cuzco. He feigned a plan to return Huáscar to the throne as Sapa Inca and declared a day for the event. He commanded the attendance of the nobles and leaders of the empire, the provincial governors and chief administrators, many of whom were related to Huáscar, indeed to Atahualpa as well. Together they comprised the *panaca*, descendants of the royal household.

The provinces of the empire had been divided since the civil war had begun. Many cities had simply continued life as usual, while others in the most remote or recently conquered reaches of the empire rebelled or simply ignored Inca rule for the time being, awaiting the outcome of events. Now that Atahualpa was victorious, and apparently in control, however, they were being called upon to declare their loyalty.

Once everyone was gathered in Cuzco, Atahualpa had them all slain, so effectively ending further resistance by destroying the *panaca's* very existence.

Yet Atahualpa went further still in his aim to eliminate the royal family: he ordered the burning of the mummy of Tupac Yupanqui, the tenth Sapa Inca and ancestor of the *panaca*.

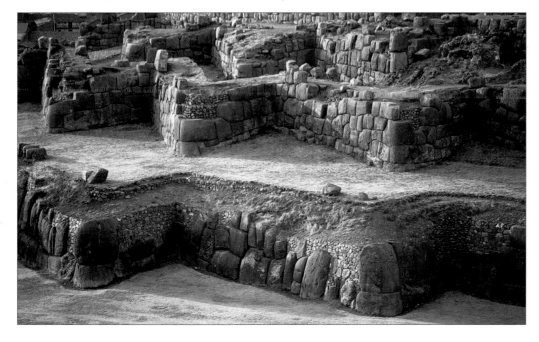

CONQUEST OF THE EMPIRE

Even before Francisco Pizarro (1475–1541) began his Andean explorations, an entire empire, that of the Aztecs, had been conquered in Mesoamerica by his countryman Hernán Cortés.

PIZARRO'S RETURN
A veteran of an expedition to Panama in 1509, Pizarro was eager to emulate Cortés. After two voyages from Panama to the South American mainland, he had returned with enough knowledge of the coast, stories of rich cities inland and to the south, and examples of gold and silver objects and textiles to convince him another civilization of great wealth lay to the south.

In 1526, had he attempted on his second expedition to invade the fringe of the Inca Empire, he would surely have been defeated. The empire was at its height under Sapa Inca Huayna Capac (1493–1526), with provincial garrisons and a strong army able to move quickly from centre to province along an efficient road system. In 1531, however, an attack

Below: The walls and defensive gateway of the fortress city of Rumicolca, about 35km (21 miles) southeast of Cuzco.

and pillaging of the coastal, provincial port of Tumbes by the inhabitants of Puná Island went unavenged, for Capac's successor, Huáscar, was otherwise engaged.

Pizarro visited Tumbes in 1526. When he returned in 1532, he still had the two native interpreters from the town, whom he had taken with him to Spain to raise royal permission and funds for his third expedition. Now the Inca Empire was in a state of turmoil. Huáscar's army had recently been defeated by his half-brother, Atahualpa, Huáscar had been captured, and Atahualpa had seized the throne.

IMPERIAL OMENS
Even before this civil war, Huayna Capac told his sons that Inti, the sun god, had informed him that his reign was the last of the twelve Sapas. Inca rule would end with the arrival of powerful strangers, whom he believed to be the foreigners recently reported arriving by sea on the north coast. Their coming was foretold by ill omens: during ceremonies honouring Inti, an eagle was mobbed and killed by buzzards and the priests prophesied disaster; and one night the new moon had three halos – one red, one black, one smoky.

Above: Francisco Pizarro, who was born illegitimate in Trujillo, Estremadura, turned from swineherd into soldier of fortune.

The priests said the red ring foretold war between the Sapa's descendants, the black ring the demise of Inti and the smoke the vanishing of the empire. These were weaknesses that Pizarro could exploit.

Huayna Capac ordered his sons to obey the strangers, for they were in every way superior. Written after the fact, the Spanish-Inca historian Garcilaso de la Vega's account appears to be a combination of political expediency and rationalization for the collapse of the empire, which the Incas believed to be perfect. In reality, weaknesses in the Inca hierarchy, civil war, the size of the empire and the shear audacity of Pizarro better explain the subsequent events.

THE MARCH TO CAJAMARCA
The arrival of reinforcements from Panama brought Pizarro's grand army to 260 men (198 foot soldiers and 62 cavalry). Tumbes had supported Huáscar in the civil war, providing a ready-made ally. Leaving a garrison in Tumbes, Pizarro marched inland with his best troops.

Left: A fanciful depiction of Atahualpa before his capture by Pizarro. Inca soldiers did not march and fight naked.

20 cavalrymen, then Hernando Pizarro with another 20, were sent to seek Atahualpa, who waited for them at his quarters, together with his court and some 400 warriors.

The Spaniards had to push their way through the Inca ranks. Accounts of the exchange vary: de Soto impressed the Incas with a display of horsemanship, then invited Atahualpa to the Spanish camp. Hernando arrived. Atahualpa declared that he was fasting and would visit on the next day. He claimed that one of his chiefs had killed three Spaniards and a horse back on the march. Hernando denied that any Inca could overcome a Spaniard. Atahualpa complained that one of his provincial chiefs had disobeyed him and Hernando bragged that ten horsemen could put down the revolt. *Chicha* was brought in large gold vessels. Etiquette was served; macho was displayed. It was left at that.

Below: Hernando Pizarro and Hernando de Soto were sent by Francisco Pizarro as envoys to Atahualpa at Cajamarca.

To win more allies, he adopted a pacific approach. He forbade looting, and encouraged his Dominican friars to convert the heathens; but opposition, where met, was put down brutally – opposing provincial chiefs were burned as examples. His campaign became a crusade.

Atahualpa marched his army – reportedly 40–50,000 warriors – nearly 1,600km (1,000 miles) to Cajamarca to await Pizarro, who was himself travelling on a litter. With 110 foot soldiers and 67 cavalrymen, Pizarro camped near Tambo Grande and sent his lieutenant, Hernando de Soto, to reconnoitre. De Soto returned with an Inca official bearing gifts and an invitation to Cajamarca. Pizarro accepted the gifts, sent the official back with gifts of his own and a message that he represented the most powerful emperor in the world, offering service against the Sapa's enemies, and continued his slow march south and east towards the 4,000m (13,000ft) pass to Cajamarca.

Atahualpa sent a gift of ten llamas. The messenger gave an account of the war with Huáscar, and Pizarro allegedly delivered a speech declaring peaceful intentions, but was prepared for war if challenged. Another day's march involved

being greeted by an Inca official with *chicha* (maize liquor) in gold cups – he was to lead the Spaniards to Cajamarca.

An allied chief whom Pizarro had sent to Atahualpa returned. He attacked Atahualpa's official, calling him a liar, and claimed that the Sapa had refused to receive him. He said that Cajamarca was deserted and Atahualpa had deployed his army on the plain ready for war. Atahualpa's ambassador retorted that Cajamarca had been vacated to make it ready for Pizarro – that it was the Sapa's custom to camp with this army on campaign (meaning the civil war). These exchanges must have left Pizarro more confused than ever.

Finally Pizarro, his men suffering from altitude sickness and exhaustion, climbed the hills into Cajamarca Valley. At any time Atahualpa could have destroyed him, yet he did nothing.

ETIQUETTE OBSERVED

Pizarro marched into Cajamarca's main courtyard on 15 November 1532, passing the vastly larger Inca army, his men arranged in three divisions to make the most of his comparatively meagre force. No envoy awaited or arrived. De Soto and

CAPTURE AND REGICIDE

Atahualpa arrived at the Spanish camp late on 16 November. There had been debate among his advisers and he had decided to visit with an armed entourage. Inca warriors lined the route and surrounding grasslands. Atahualpa, carried by his chiefs on a litter adorned with gold and silver plates, was preceded by elite warriors in colourful chequered livery, singing, dancing and sweeping the roadway before him. Atahualpa himself was bedecked with gold and turquoise jewellery, and the entire retinue displayed his wealth and majesty.

The journey was less than 6km (4 miles), yet Atahualpa hesitated, sent a messenger that he would come the next day, then changed his mind and resumed progress, now with only 6,000 unarmed followers. Atahualpa's indecision revealed a lack of human confidence despite his obsession with displaying his dignity and status as a living god. He simply could not understand the nature of the men he was dealing with.

SLAUGHTER AND CAPTURE
Entering the empty courtyard, Atahualpa was greeted by Pizarro's friar, Valverde, brandishing a Bible and a crucifix. He delivered a discourse on Christianity.

Left: In early meetings with Atahualpa's noble ambassadors, Francisco Pizarro and Hernando De Soto professed peace.

Historians will forever remain unsure of the ensuing events. Despite the message having to pass through an interpreter, it seems clear that Atahualpa understood what was being demanded of him: renunciation of everything he believed in, of his entire world. Allegedly, Valverde handed him the Bible; allegedly he threw it down, pointing at the sun and declaring 'My God still lives.'

Valverde retrieved the Bible and retreated. Pizarro gave the signal to attack: a cannon was fired into the crowd, followed by arquebuses (long-barrelled guns); then his men charged. Atahualpa's chiefs fought with bare hands to save their emperor, and were butchered in the attempt. A wall collapsed in the frenzy of retreating natives. Those trapped in the courtyard were slaughtered until night fell and Atahualpa was taken captive. Thus treachery was accomplished. It must have seemed to Pizarro that this was the only way to succeed against clearly overwhelming odds. The chronicler Zárete records that the whole plot had been discussed and decided the night before. Pizarro had indeed emulated Cortés by taking the emperor hostage.

GREED AND BETRAYAL
The passivity of Atahualpa's people and army is astounding. They simply melted away, leaving their possessions in camp. The Spaniards looted Cajamarca and the chiefs' tents, seized the army's llama herds and raped the women abandoned in the royal baths.

The remainder of the story is equally sordid. Realizing Pizarro's lust for gold and silver, Atahualpa offered to fill the 5.5 by 7m (18 by 23ft) room in which he was held, as high as he could reach, with gold. Pizarro demanded that, in addition, the adjoining smaller room be filled twice

Above: Having captured Atahualpa at Cajamarca, Pizarro imprisoned him in a palace room while a ransom was negotiated.

with silver. Atahualpa agreed to these demands, asked for two months, and ordered the collection of gold and silver objects from all over the empire.

At Atahualpa's request, three Spaniards, including de Soto, were sent to Cuzco to hasten the collections. They found the captive Huáscar, who offered to treble his half-brother's ransom. Learning this, Atahualpa gave secret orders for Huáscar to be murdered.

In January 1533, Hernando was sent on an expedition to Pachacamac. In April, Diego de Almagro and reinforcements arrived from Panama. Pizarro bided his time, while his soldiers grew restless – they had come for conquest and spoils.

There remained the problem of Atahualpa. Despite incomplete fulfilment of his agreement, Pizarro absolved him of further obligation, but still held him – 'for security'. He was now an encumbrance; Pizarro wanted power and Atahualpa, now only a rallying point for native rebellion, stood in his way. De Almagro and his men wanted action and plunder. Rumours of native insurrection, the 'demands' of his

men and the Spanish Inquisition provided Pizarro with justification for a 'trial'. He and de Almagro were the judges. Atahualpa was accused of usurpation of the Inca throne and the murder of Huáscar the true heir, of inciting insurrection, of distributing gold and silver that should have been used to fulfil his ransom agreement and of adultery – as Sapas had numerous wives – and idolatry. He was convicted and condemned to be burned at the stake.

THE END OF INCA RULE

The final shameless act in these procedures followed. Twelve captains called the affair a travesty of justice, but were persuaded of its political expediency. When Atahualpa realized that he was to be burned, he agreed to be baptized a

Right: Despite this image, Atahualpa was strangled to death, after becoming a Christian to avoid being burned at the stake.

Christian for the favour of strangulation, for if he were burned, in Inca belief he would be condemned in afterlife, unable to be mummified and to continue to participate in life.

Pizarro finally marched to Cuzco and established Spanish government – a year after the events in Cajamarca. Alleged plans for insurrection by Challcuchima, one of Atahualpa's own generals, 'justified' his execution. A puppet Sapa, Manco, another of Huayna Capac's sons, was crowned. The last of Atahualpa's generals, Quizquiz, was defeated and fled to Quito, where he was killed by his own men.

The first years of Spanish rule were fraught with embittered rivalry between Pizarro, de Almagro and others. Pizarro enjoyed power for a mere eight years before being assassinated by rivals.

Below: The alleged 'ransom room' in Inca Cajamarca in which Atahualpa was imprisoned after being captured.

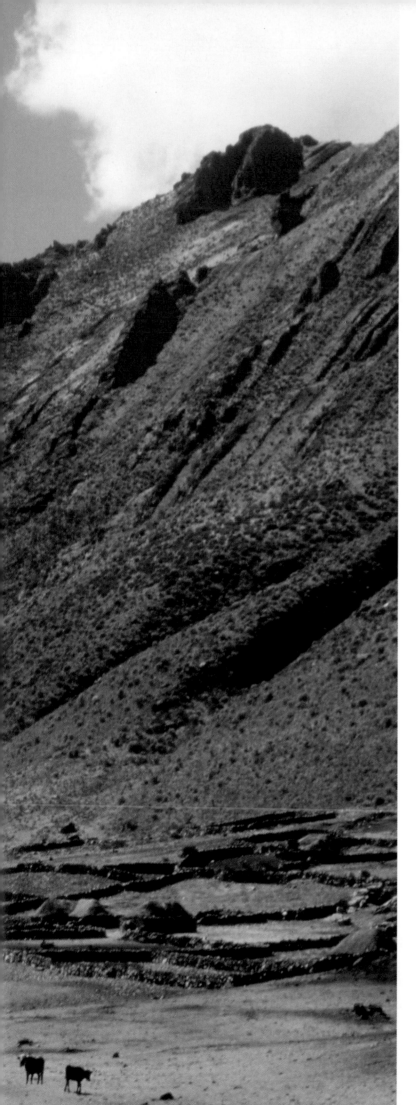

CHAPTER TWO

THE LAND

The continent of South America has a geography of extremes. Its mountains are some of the highest in the world – up to 7,000m (23,000ft); its deserts are some of the driest; its rainforests some of the wettest and densest; and its western offshore seas – the Humboldt Current – teem with some of the most abundant fisheries. Climates range from damp, steaming jungles to cold, dry deserts, and from cool, high plains to lofty, oxygen-rare summits. Rainfall can range from near zero to as much as 8,000mm (315in) a year.

Within this continent lies the Andean Area, which includes the two Cordilleras of the Andes, bordering the Amazon Rainforest on one side and the Atacama and other deserts on the other. Here humans have had to adapt to life at high altitudes. South of the Cordillera lies the Altiplano, where much of the area's farming is carried out. Here potatoes and other root crops were grown, and large herds of llamas kept for their wool. To the west lie coastal valleys and oases within the desert, where a variety of crops were grown.

East of the Andes is another world. The eastern mountain flanks descend more gradually through forested slopes, known as *montaña*, to the low, hot tropical forests, known as the selva. Here human settlement was more dispersed, yet products of the rainforest remained prominent in Andean and western coastal cultures throughout history.

Despite such extremes and a land of independent settlements, the Incas did not live in isolation: rather trade and social contact linked the settlements in both highlands and lowlands.

Left: The Callejon de Huaylas in north-central Peru epitomizes the sweeping slopes and high sierra valleys of the Andes.

PEAKS AND MOUNTAIN VALLEYS

The Andean Cordillera has been shaped in two distinct ways: by the movement of tectonic plates and by the weather.

FORMATION OF THE ANDES

Nearly two million years ago, the westward-moving South American continental plate met the eastward-moving Nazca ocean plate along the Pacific coast, moving at up to 15cm (6in) a year. The ocean plate, which has a heavier stone composition, was pushed beneath the lighter and less dense continental plate. Friction and drag where the two plates met caused folding, which created the Andean mountain chain. Where the ocean plate melted from the friction, the sedimentary rocks cracked, hurling molten rocks to the surface as volcanoes.

Below: Llamas, alpacas and vicuñas helped Andean civilizations to develop and survive in the Altiplano and high mountains.

Along their widest stretch, the spine of the Andes comprises two parallel ridges. On the east, the higher Cordillera Blanca borders the Amazon Rainforest. On the west, the Cordillera Negra fronts the Atacama Desert. South of this broad range the ridges diverge to flank, east and west, the broad Altiplano; to the north the mountains split into several ridges running parallel to the main ranges, and are cross-cut by shorter ridges to frame numerous sierra basins and valleys known as *puna*.

EFFECTS OF THE WEATHER

The distant Atlantic Ocean is the source of most of South America's precipitation. Westward-moving rain and snow meet the high Andes and fall on the eastern escarpments. West of the Andes, which lies in the rain shadow, a more arid Pacific weather pattern predominates. The Andes become drier as they become higher, and the Altiplano around the drainage of the

Above: In the challenging terrain of the sierra valleys and basins, rivers provided the vital water needed for agriculture.

Lake Titicaca basin forms a huge region of uninterrupted agricultural flatlands. Ninety per cent of Andean drainage runs east, ultimately to the Atlantic. Ten per cent drains into the Pacific, in numerous short, east–west-running river valleys from the western Andean flank.

The Andes also deflect prevailing ocean winds to blow north, causing the Pacific to flow northwards along the coast. Upwelling water from the deep tectonic trench brings cold, nutrient-rich and therefore seafood-rich currents, but also chills the air, so causing sparse rainfall.

A CHALLENGING ENVIRONMENT

The mountainous and highland regions of the Andes provide one of the most challenging environments on earth to their inhabitants. High mountain ecosystems are characteristically of low productivity, yet the majority of people in the central Andes live above 2,500m (8,200ft). Such altitudes comprise steep-sided valleys and basins, rugged terrains and a generally fragile landscape. Limited flat agricultural land, poor soils and a short growing season make production difficult. In addition, low oxygen levels, infrequent rainfall, high winds, high solar radiation and prevailing cold temperatures make survival tenuous.

Above: Mt Ausangate, in the central Peruvian Cordillera, was a typical abode of apu *spirits: sacred deities who inhabited the peaks.*

ADAPTING TO ALTITUDE

The high altitude causes stress on all life forms, and in humans, in particular, it decreases blood oxygen saturation by up to 30 per cent, which means breathing can be difficult for the unaccustomed. Andean peoples' bodies have, of course, become adapted to these conditions, with large chest cavities and lung capacity. Their cellular metabolism has modified to sustain higher red blood cell numbers. Nevertheless, strenuous work demands more energy to sustain the raised breathing, circulation and metabolic rates needed to maintain body temperature. As a result, highland peoples need to eat more to maintain a high basic metabolic rate, yet ironically they live in an environment where it is difficult to produce and obtain the necessary food for this diet.

The peopling of the Andes was thus a slow process, with generations at one altitude gradually becoming adapted to life at that level before their descendants could move into the next, higher zone, where the adaptive process took place again. Europeans, for the most part from comparatively lowland environments, have still been adapting through the generations since colonization began.

Unfortunately, we have no records of how lowland South Americans fared or coped with the high altitudes. Comparisons of the skeletons from lowland and highland burials, however, show that the two populations were more related within than between their respective groups.

POTATOES AND LLAMAS

In these highlands, agriculture consisted of a combination of root crops and herding. Because there are relatively few sizeable valleys – the valleys around Cuzco being exceptions – the steep slopes of valley and basin sides had to be adapted to provide flat areas for cultivation. Considerable labour and expertise were devoted to building millions of hillside terraces (*andenes*) and networks of irrigation canals.

The staple highland crop was the potato. Beans, squashes, peppers and peanuts were also important food crops. Maize can be grown at altitudes of up to 3,300m (11,000ft), but is at great risk from frost and hail at such heights.

The only domesticated animals were camelids (llamas, alpacas and vicuñas), dogs, guinea pigs and ducks. Llamas were herded in great flocks and provided the only pack animals for transport. They were also used for their wool (as were alpacas), meat and medicine. Dogs were raised as hunting companions and for food. Guinea pigs and ducks were raised for food, and also eggs in the case of the latter.

Below: Geographic map of the Andean Area, showing coastal plains, the Andes and the eastern rainforest.

ABUNDANT PLAINS – THE ALTIPLANO

The vast Altiplano (high plain) south of the central Peruvian Andes is formed where the principal Cordillera Blanca and Cordillera Negra diverge. Centred towards Lake Titicaca at the present Peruvian–Bolivian border, it lies at nearly 4,000m (13,000ft) above sea level. It forms a long trough, 800km (500 miles) north-west to south-east and drains north to south through a chain of lakes from Lake Azangaro in Peru through Titicaca to Lake Poopó in Bolivia. It is the largest expanse of agricultural flatlands in the Andean Area. The depth (up to 200m/650ft) and expanse (8,600 sq km/3,320 sq miles) of Lake Titicaca provides, as do the other lakes, a moderating influence on local temperatures.

In much of this region there was less need for labour-intensive terracing. Instead, pre-Hispanic peoples developed several methods for intensifying agricultural

Below: The high plains of the southern Andean plateaux are punctuated by volcanic cones, such as El Misti, believed to be the homes of gods whose destructive powers were feared.

Above: The sparser, bleaker high plains of the southern Altiplano provide little scope for agriculture, but they were widely used for llama herding.

production. Rivers were tapped by canals dug to channel their waters into the fields and to regulate ground water levels. In addition, check dams were constructed to collect and store run-off water, and aqueducts and dikes were made to divert and distribute it among the fields to water the crops.

CLAIMING THE LAND

During periods of high precipitation, the large region of low land, relatively speaking, around Lake Titicaca and the other lakes was reclaimed for agriculture by creating long, wide, ridged fields of mounded soils. They were separated by channels of slow-moving water, which provided protection from frost by releasing overnight the heat they had absorbed from the sun during the day. Nevertheless, to help maintain dense population levels, the steep slopes of the surrounding hills were also terraced to provide extra agricultural fields.

In drought years, when the lake level could drop by as much as 12m (39ft), some 50,000ha (124,000 acres) of formerly

Above: Alpacas were a species closely related to the llama. They provided a finer grade of wool than the llama.

cultivated land were left without the usual water channels and were simply abandoned temporarily.

As in the *puna*, the principal crops of the Altiplano were root vegetables. There were multiple varieties of potato, various tubers, legumes and grains such as quinoa domesticated from regional native species. In addition, the lakes, and especially Titicaca, provided a rich variety of aquatic resources. The deep, cold waters of the lakes supported abundant fish stocks, which had been exploited from early times. Migrating waterfowl (ducks and flamingos) provided plenty of seasonal meat and eggs. The shallow lakeshores harboured edible reeds – also used for roof thatching, clothing and for making fishing boats, and various water plants provided animal forage and were gathered as fodder for domesticated llama herds and guinea pigs.

GREAT HERDS OF LLAMAS

The llama and alpaca were both cornerstones of the Altiplano economy. Great herds of them were especially kept in the southern and northern Altiplano to sustain a pastoral way of life. From being the hunting grounds of the earliest inhabitants, these grasslands became the focus of llama and alpaca domestication from as early as 5000BC. Throughout the Andean

Area they were bred carefully for multiple purposes. The primary reason was for their wool, providing woven textiles for clothing, hats, bags and slings, as well as for exchange with lowland settlements for their produce. Textiles were also used to fulfil social taxation obligations.

As well as wool, several by-products were also of value. Llama meat and fat were important sources of protein and energy. Their bones were made into many tools, from scrapers, knives, needles and awls to musical instruments. The hides were made into clothing and other articles. Their dung was used as fuel and provided a source of fertilizer to re-enrich fields left fallow between growing seasons. Whole llamas were frequently sacrificed in religious ceremonies, and figured prominently in Andean cosmology. Finally, they were the pick-up trucks of pre-Hispanic Andeans, used to transport commodities over long distances.

Below: Vicuñas were prized for their fine wool and have adapted to high altitudes, where drought and freezing nights are the rule.

Above: Llamas were valuable, sure-footed pack animals for transporting goods between highlands and lowlands.

LIFE AT THE EDGE

Beyond the Altiplano lake basins, and especially towards the southern extreme of the great trough that forms the Altiplano, the landscape becomes increasingly arid. It would have been unsuitable for agriculture, or even llama herding, except in various isolated areas where a tenuous growing season could have been exploited with careful irrigation.

WESTERN DESERTS AND COASTAL VALLEYS

The western descent to the coastal strip of the Andean Area was an important and rich area of isolated cultural oases, at least in earliest pre-Hispanic times.

The region's climate is controlled by the Humboldt Current, which brings cold water northwards along the coast and creates cool, arid conditions inland. While the coastal air remains humid, causing coastal fog, temperature inversion (whereby air decreases in temperature less quickly than usual as it climbs) over the land inhibits rainfall and creates deserts inland – chiefly the Sechura in the north and the Atacama in the south of the Andean Area.

There is more arable land in the northern coastal valleys than in the southern coastal area. From north to south. there are three climate zones: semi-tropical in the north, sub-tropical in the middle and sub-tropical to desert in the south. The principal pre-Hispanic products of the coastal valleys and desert oases were maize, beans, squashes, peanuts, manioc, avocado and other semi-tropical fruits, and cotton.

Above: Eroding salt deposits of ancient raised shorelines are seen here at San Pedro de Atacama in Chile, the driest desert environment in the world.

IRRIGATION SYSTEMS

Along the Pacific watershed of the coastal strip virtually all desert farming and 85 per cent of sierra–coastal valley agriculture is reliant on run-off irrigation. More than 60 short rivers, rising in the steep western Andean slopes, descend through rugged then quickly levelling terrain to the Pacific Ocean. Tapping them for their water involved elaborate, labour-intensive projects to dig canals and channels to bring water from distant rivers to terraced fields. The very nature and sophistication of such works encouraged different regions to work together to establish and maintain them.

In the southern region of the coastal strip large expanses of desert provided a different challenge. Here people needed to bring water from the nearby sierra and from more widely spaced rivers. The Nazca and other rivers in this region flow on the surface in the upper

Left: Off-shore islands, such as Ballesta Island, Peru, were valuable sources of guano, used as fertilizer and a valuable trade item.

valleys only; down-valley they disappear into subterranean channels. In response to this condition, and perhaps enhanced in times of drought, the peoples of the area built elaborate underground irrigation systems of aqueducts to bring water from the underground rivers and to gather the water table through an arrangement of trenches and tunnels into catchment cisterns that could be tapped when needed.

HARVESTING THE SEA

In addition to agriculture, especially in the northern valleys (and largely independently from the southern desert valley agricultural societies), coastal cultures exploited the extremely rich maritime resources of the Pacific. Molluscs and crustaceans were collected on the foreshore; large and small fish were taken in nets and by hook (anchovies and sardines were harvested throughout the year and seasonally, respectively); sea mammals were hunted with harpoons; and sea birds were regularly taken. Offshore

islands, havens for vast seabird colonies, provided a regular source of guano for fertilizing the fields. Even edible kelp leaves were collected as a food source.

One commodity sought from farther north was the bivalve *Spondylus princeps* – the spiny or thorny oyster. Native in the coastal waters from Ecuador north to Baja California, it was exploited by coastal peoples from as early as 3000BC. Its collection is not easy, because its habitat is

Above: Vast deserts along the coasts of Peru and northern Chile contained scores of river valleys, providing oases for early agriculture.

18–50m (60–160ft) deep. Nevertheless, divers regularly collected it, and throughout pre-Hispanic times it provided a rich source of coastal and inland trade to both the north and south. It was sought as a ritual object and provides evidence of long-distance trade and contact between different cultures.

OASES CULTURES

In times of drought, oases cultures were stretched severely and it required, besides their religious beliefs, fortitude and ingenuity to sustain their cultural ways. Each river supplying an oasis valley, desert oasis or western sierra basin was otherwise isolated. Such isolation enabled several nearly self-governing populations to arise and maintain their independence. At the same time, however, there was a need for contact and the trading of goods from one region to another. Such links between desert oases, and indeed valleys, were spiritual and military enterprises whose strengths waxed and waned throughout Andean Area history.

Left: Ancient peoples of the desert coastlands relied on the rich harvest of the sea, and traded exotic shells with highland cultures.

49

THE *MONTAÑA* AND EASTERN RAINFORESTS

The geography of the eastern flank of the Altiplano and Cordillera provides a complete contrast to the western Cordillera. Here there are high, bleak plateaux called the *montaña* or Ceja de Selva, where the terrain and vegetation make agriculture difficult and careful terracing and water management are necessary. Llama herding is widespread here. Starting at about 4,000m (13,000ft) above sea level, the *montañas*, known as cloud forests, drop towards the east until they merge with true tropical forest. Rainfall averages 2,000–4,000mm (80–160in) a year.

RAINFOREST PRODUCTS

In addition to llama products, the hard and soft woods of the slopes provided the only major source of timber and wood for everyday and religious objects in the Andean Area. Agriculture on the middle slopes included maize, beans, squash, peanuts, peppers and cotton, all of which were transported by llama caravans specially commissioned by the rulers and elite of the Altiplano.

Most importantly, the *montaña* was the source of coca *(Erythroxylon coca)*, used for both practical and spiritual purposes. The alkaloid compounds derived from

Below: The stealth and power of the jaguar was revered by Andean peoples. It was a common 'form' for shape-changing shamans.

Above: The dense rainforests of Antisuyu were the source of many products, including hallucinogenic mushrooms.

the dried leaves of the coca plant or shrub provided (and continue to provide today) stimulation to relieve the fatigue of strenuous labour at high altitudes. It was also a ritual commodity of symbolic and real importance from very early times. Its importance and limited availability also encouraged political arrangements and even wars over its control. The true tropical rainforest lies mostly outside the Andean Area. Here precipitation can be in excess of 8,000mm (315in) per year, and it flows into rivers destined for the Atlantic Ocean. However, both the eastern *montaña* descending from the Altiplano and the north-eastern slopes from the northern Andes meet the Amazon Rainforest.

This closeness of *montaña* and rainforest encouraged cultural links, trade for rainforest products and a reverence for its creatures. The red, blue and yellow feathers of rainforest parrots, kingfishers and macaws were coveted by highland peoples. Harpy eagle feathers were also sought, and the bird's predatory nature admired. Cayman and serpent representations featured in much highland art and religious iconography, starting with the Chavín culture. Gold collected in placer mines, hallucinogenic plants (especially mushrooms and tobacco), resinous woods and various tropical fruits and medicinal plants all made their way to Andean cities. Jaguar pelts and monkeys were sought as both were revered animals whose cunning, courage, fierceness and cleverness was to be emulated.

THE LIMITS OF CIVILIZATION
The eastern boundaries of the Inca Empire extended to the edges of the Amazon. To the Incas this was the land of the Antisuyu quarter and the eastern edge of Collasuyu quarter, the place where civilization ended and savagery began. It was Inca Roca, the sixth Inca ruler, who defeated the Chunchos of Antisuyu only by adopting their savage tropical forest methods of fighting – he 'became' a jaguar and wore a green cloak. Viracocha, the eighth Sapa Inca, established the boundary between civilized highlands and savage Antisuyu when he destroyed the town of Calca 'with a fireball', 'propelling' it to the other side of the River Vilcanota. Manco Capac, the founding Inca – who was defined in legend as carrying maize, the highland, civilized crop – defeated the Hualla Indians in the Cuzco Valley. They were described as growers of rainforest crops such as peppers and coca.

The Incas made several attempts to conquer parts of the rainforest, but the environment proved too alien. Once within the forest, Inca generals lacked familiar points of reference on a visible horizon and their disorientated armies thrashed about in the dense, unfamiliar terrain. Pachacuti Inca Yupanqui, Tupac Yupanqui and Huayna Capac all sent campaigns into the jungles, and all were defeated. Despite this, bowmen from the *montaña* and tropical forest borders were recruited into the Inca army.

Above: Exotic rainforest birds provided the colourful feathers for ritual capes, tunics and headdresses made by skilled craftsmen.

A PLACE APART
To the Inca, the rainforest was *hurin*, feminine and subservient, despite their failure to conquer any of it or coerce any of its inhabitants into taxable submission. Ollantaytambo and Machu Picchu in Antisuyu defined the edge of Inca civilization, and one of their purposes in their border positions was to attempt to control coca production.

The trading relationship between highland cultures and tropical forest peoples was mostly one-way: from the tropical forest to the highlands. Although trade, both in commodities and ideas, was brisk at the borders, no serious attempts were made by highland peoples to colonize the rainforest or to establish large trading settlements at the borders. The rainforests remained in this passive role throughout pre-Hispanic history, providing precious raw materials, imagery and inspiration, but otherwise remaining a separate world.

Left: Winding rivers in the rainforest were home to the cayman, the South American crocodile, which inspired religious images.

LAND OF EXTREMES

The Andean Cordillera occupied by the Incas and their predecessors is an area of extremes, both environmental and ecological. They include the full global range of geographic landscapes and seascapes, from dense rainforests to teaming oceans. The Cordillera's inhabitants would have had to cope with fundamental contrasts in terrain, soil, water resources, sea, weather and temperature, depending on where they settled. Characteristically, though frustratingly for farmers, where there is adequate level land for cultivation there is often little water, and vice versa. Equally, seasonal and cyclical weather patterns mean that periods of regular rainfall, producing fertile growing conditions, are interspersed with periods of drought sometimes lasting years, decades or even centuries.

IRREGULAR RAINFALL

The mountainous landscape of the Cordillera means that rainfall is irregularly distributed. It is seasonal, starting about late October and November, climaxing between December and March and virtually disappearing from June to September. This annual cycle is decidedly irregular, however, swinging between values above and below the median, which occurs only about once every four years. This irregularity introduces another paradox in Andean survival. Rainfall for higher-altitude agriculture, where farmers devised methods to make more cultivatable land available, but where there is less water, generally fluctuates less. Yet run-off agriculture, which is generally more productive, is possible mostly where the rainfall fluctuates the most.

Highland farming is most successful when rainfall is heavy enough to cause sufficient run-off for crop production. (The run-off is stored in a structure of suitable size and construction and used to water the land during dry periods.) But arid mountain soils absorb fixed amounts of moisture, and so run-off occurs only when this absorption level is exceeded. Rainfall exceeding this capacity generally occurs only between about 3,900m (12,800ft) and 4,900m (16,100ft). Above about 5,000m (16,400ft) most available water is locked-up in glaciers and ice fields. Therefore, severe fluctuations in rainfall in this crucial altitudinal zone have a severe effect on the amount of

Above: The Incas conquered the parched, desiccated surface of the Atacama and other western coastal deserts.

run-off water available down-slope in the most important agricultural basins and valleys. This unbalanced relationship between rainfall and run-off also explains the dramatic variation of the rivers of the Pacific coastal valleys.

STRESSFUL CONDITIONS

The effects of living at high altitude and coping with low blood oxygen saturation made life stressful for early Andeans. They needed to eat more than lowlanders to maintain their metabolic rate, yet changeable weather patterns and scarce foodstuffs made life precarious. Supporting and sustaining civilization in highland regions was thus measurably more costly in many ways than it was in lowland areas.

Alongside the daily stresses of living, earth movements and weather cycles caused problems. Tectonic activity, both small and large scale, brings disastrous consequences. Relentless tectonic creep exacerbates erosional patterns and affects canals and water collection methods by altering slopes, damaging canals and affecting their performance.

Left: The lush, well-watered Amazonian rainforest proved to be too alien and disorientating to the Inca armies.

Sudden disaster also came from earthquakes and volcanoes. Shifts from the plates that formed the Andes brought an earthquake of magnitude 7 or greater on the Richter Scale about once a decade. The immediate effects and consequent landslides caused fatalities as well as damage to buildings, canals and other structures. Volcanic activity persisted throughout ancient times, and into the present, especially in the northern Andean Area in Ecuador, southern Colombia and the Vicanota region of southern Peru.

Unable to explain these events scientifically, peoples of the Andes developed their own spiritual explanations involving cosmic battles and angry gods. Even into modern times they believed in mountain gods. When Mount Huaynaputina in southern Peru erupted in AD1600, the power of the explosion blew the entire crown of the mountain away, leaving a huge crater. Natives believed the event to be a rebellion of the ancient deities against the victory of the Christian gods.

Below: The sierra valleys were well watered but challenging. Raised fields and terracing maximized the amount of level ground for crops.

THE DREADED EL NIÑO

The phenomenon known as El Niño disrupted even what could be regarded as the 'regular' rainfall cycles described above, introducing perennial episodes of hostsile weather conditions. El Niños occur about every four to ten years. They are caused by the warming of the eastern tropical Pacific, changing atmospheric conditions, and altering weather cycles in the far and central Pacific. The conditions

Above: The high sierra provided abundant water for mountain valleys and oases, as well as mountain gods and burial places.

also act to magnify the effects of changes in solar radiation. Usually lasting about 18 months, El Niños generate torrential storms accompanied by cataclysmic floods along the western coasts. Simultaneously, because the weather patterns have been reversed, the mountains and Altiplano become subject to prolonged periods of drought.

Along the desert western coasts, tonnes of debris deposited by earthquake-induced landslides, having lain loose for years, are flushed into the sea in the floods. Ground into fine sands by wave action, it is redeposited along the beaches. Strong offshore winds then collect it into huge dunes that can choke the life out of cities and settlements far inland.

Even longer-term droughts and wet periods affected Cordillera civilization. Evidence from glacier ice shows a substantial increase in atmospheric dust caused by drought between c.2200 and 1900BC; other extended droughts occurred in 900–800BC, 400–200BC, AD1–300, 562–95 and 1100–1450. Wetter periods occurred in AD400–500, 900–100 and 1500–1700.

PLACES OF WORSHIP

To the Incas, and no doubt to their Andean Area ancestors, their entire surroundings were sacred. Throughout the landscape, special places that had been revered for generation after generation, and where offerings were made or special rituals performed, were known as *huacas*. As well as the powerful central deities of the Inca pantheon, whose presences were manifested in individual temples in the Coricancha in Cuzco, Andean peoples recognized a host of lesser nature gods, spirits and oracles that existed throughout the land. *Huacas* were places where such lesser figures could also be revered and, if necessary, placated.

INCA *HUACAS*

Huacas were hallowed places where significant mythological events had taken place and/or where offerings were made to local deities. It is thought that all Andean cultures had *huacas* that were special to them, and thus most *huacas* were of ancient origin. The majority were natural

Below: The sacred Intihuatana (Hitching Post of the Sun) at Machu Picchu typifies natural outcrops carved as sacred huacas.

features of the landscape, such as mountaintops (*apus*), caves, springs and especially stones or boulders, but they could also be man-made objects, or natural objects or landscape features modified by human workmanship. An Inca *huaca* could also be a location along a sacred *ceque* line (a sacred route), such as the pillars erected on the western horizon above Cuzco for viewing the sunset from the Capac Usnu for special astronomical observations.

In and around Cuzco there were more than 300 *huacas*. Other Inca sacred places were concentrated wherever there was an association with a ruler. For example, Huayna Capac, the twelfth Sapa Inca, undertook a special pilgrimage to visit the favourite places of his father, Tupac Yupanqui, in Cajamarca, as did Atahualpa those of Huayna Capac in the northern provinces before marching against his brother Huáscar. Ironically, it was in Cajamarca that Atahualpa met defeat at the hands of Pizarro.

Ceque lines themselves, by their very nature as sacred or ritual pathways, were also *huacas*, and, equally, they incorporated *huacas* as points along the sacred routes they provided.

Above: The outcrop of Qenqo, north of Cuzco, was one of the Inca's most sacred huacas. *It resembles a seated puma.*

ANCESTRAL *HUACAS*

Royal and elite mausoleums, where the mummified remains of ancestors were kept, were also regarded as *huacas*. Spanish colonial sources identify many Inca royal *huacas*; and Chan Chan, the capital of the rulers of Chimú, surrounded their royal mausoleum compounds. These records reveal what appear to be the two basic classifications of such man-made *huacas*: the *huacas adatorios* – the sanctuaries and temples where gods and goddesses were worshipped; and the *huacas sepulturas* – the burial places of the most important members of the deceased.

A characteristic *huaca* is the collection of stones known as the Pururaucas around Cuzco. These were revered as the re-petrified ancient stones that had allegedly risen up and become Inca warriors to help Pachacuti Inca Yupanqui defend Cuzco against the Chancas in the early 15th century. Other examples include Qenqo, just north of Cuzco, where one large

Above: Stone cairns on mountain passes were a special type of huaca *called an* apacheta. *They were thought to hold local deities' spirits.*

upright boulder was left untouched, presumably because its silhouette resembled that of a seated puma, and the sacred shrines and statues of Viracocha at Cacha and Urcos. In some cases a *huaca* was a combination of the natural and the miraculous. Once again the stones of Pururaucas are a prime example. Another is the stone of the ancestor brother Ayar Uchu atop Huanacauri Mountain, which is believed to be the petrified body of that ancestor. Yet another example is Pariacaca, which/who seems to have been simultaneously a mountain and a mobile deity or culture hero.

PROVINCIAL *HUACAS*
The movements and final resting places of important rulers strengthened attachments to the natural symbolism of *huacas* as ancestral or 'parental'. The hill called Huanacauri above Cuzco, for example, was regarded as the father of three of the founding Inca ancestors, each turned to stone as a prominent rock or crag. Other Andean

peoples regarded the local mountains as being 'like parents' who gave birth to the local community. Indeed, such beliefs are enshrined in the story of the creation of peoples by the god Viracocha, who assigned each people their region as a sacred act.

Most tribes, 'nations' and towns undoubtedly had a particular place that was recognized as their group's *huaca*. Equally, most kinship groups, the *ayllus*, also had their own *huacas*. It was believed that the spirit of the *huaca* exerted a special influence over the lives and destinies of the members of the group. *Huacas* continue to be recognized by local peoples in the Andes today in a mixture of pre-Christian and Catholic belief.

LINKS FROM PAST TO PRESENT
Reverence at *huacas* and the following of *ceque* lines represented a strengthening of the past, a reassurance of the present and an insuring of the future. Indeed, the myth-history attached to Inca sacred places infused the very landscape.

The stories attached to individual *huacas* have survived mostly in fragments. Many are recoverable, however, from traditions transcribed in the longer narratives

of Inca history. Although the sacred *huaca* system is well known in and around Cuzco, there is less surviving direct evidence of other local shrines; but much may still be discovered through further research.

Below: All rivers and lakes were held sacred by ancient Andeans because water was universally recognized as the source of life.

LINES IN THE DESERT

The coastal desert *pampa* of southern Peru was the home of the Nazca culture, which flourished from about 200BC to AD500. All aspects of Nazca culture were dominated by ritual. Perhaps the most dramatic evidence of this was the making of lines and images in the desert in the form of geoglyphs. Many people have investigated the lines and their meaning over decades, including Paul Kosok, Maria Reiche and Anthony Aveni.

Other line figures were made in the Pacific coastal valleys from Lambayeque to northern Chile.

SHAPES IN THE DESERT

The Nazca desert lines are the most famous examples of pre-Inca sacred routes. The lines, which can be best seen and most appreciated from the air, were made by scraping the patinated desert surface gravel and stones to one side to reveal the lighter coloured, unpatinated under-surface. The lines are formed by

Below: The sacred route at Cantalloc on the Nazca Desert plain of southern Peru typifies a geometric geoglyph in its spiral pathway.

the combination of light sand and aligned gravel and stones. The region's natural aridity has helped to preserve them.

More than 640 sq km (425 sq miles) of the desert are covered with these lines, figures and shapes. They comprise recognizable figures, geometrical shapes and seemingly random lines and cleared areas. Recognizable figures are of animals revered in the Nazca religious concept of the world – spiders, monkeys and birds – plus flowers and human-like supernatural figures. Some lines run perfectly straight

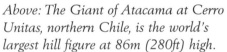

Above: The Giant of Atacama at Cerro Unitas, northern Chile, is the world's largest hill figure at 86m (280ft) high.

for great distances across the desert. Others spiral, or converge on a single point. Altogether there are some 1,300km (800 miles) of such lines.

FIGURES AND PATTERNS

There are two principal types or groups. Figures on low slopes or hillsides seem to be placed such that they are obvious to travellers on the plains below, even though seen obliquely. Patterns of lines, both straight and curving, form 'enclosed', or designated areas, geometric shapes and large cleared patches.

Sets of lines form geometric patterns, and clusters of straight lines converge on common nodes, or, conversely, radiate from 'ray centres' on hills. In his researches, the archaeo-astronomer Anthony Aveni has identified and mapped 62 such nodes and radiations. Some of the lines lead to irrigated oases, or link sites, such as the line between the settlement of Ventilla and the ritual centre of Cahuachi. Individual straight lines of various widths are more than 20km (12½ miles) long. One famous set of lines, which forms a huge arrow of 490m (roughly 1,600ft), pointing towards the Pacific Ocean, is thought to be a symbol to invoke rain.

Each animal or plant figure comprises a single continuous line, with different beginning and ending points. The line never crosses itself. There is a hummingbird, a duckling, a spider, a killer whale, a monkey, a llama, several plants and human-like beings, as well as trapezoids and triangles of cleared areas, zigzags and spirals. Altogether there are some 300 such figures, and, combined with the lines, about 3.6 million sq m (10.8 million sq ft) of *pampa* floor have been scraped away to create them.

MYSTERIOUS LINES?

The Nazca figures are difficult to conceive, and certainly impossible to see as whole figures from the ground, except obliquely. Their presence has prompted a variety of speculation regarding their meaning, and argument has raged for more than 60 years over the meanings of these and other geoglyphs. Proposals range from their having been made by beings from outer space – for which there is categorically no evidence – to their use for astronomical observation – which seems plausible but has not yet been conclusively demonstrated.

There is no evidence that the lines were made by anyone other than the Nazca themselves. Although we will never know the exact meaning of each line or figure, they are clearly ritual lines,

Below: The great hummingbird geoglyph on the Nazca Desert plain represents a messenger from the gods.

shapes and figures that reflect Nazca religious concepts. Their similarity to patterns on pottery and textiles, associations with Nazca burials and mummification, and with Nazca settlements and water sources reflects Nazca cosmology.

Creating the lines was a simple matter of proportional geometry. There is no difficulty in tracing an envisioned figure in the sand, and then translating the shape into a giant figure on the ground: only multiplication and proportional ratios are necessary to replicate a drawing using strings and pegs to trace and pace out the positions of the lines and patterns. Straight lines that cross the desert are easily produced by aiming at fixed positions on the horizon. Practical experiments to make neo-Nazca lines have proved the ease with which they can be created and the relatively small number of people and time needed to do so.

WHAT WERE THEY USED FOR?

The most plausible, and indeed obvious, explanation of the meaning of the Nazca lines is linked to the landscape, climate and accompanying features of Nazca settlement and material culture. The lines were associated with the Nazcas' necessary preoccupation with water and the fertility of their crops, together with the worship of mountains – the ultimate source of irrigation waters – and a pantheon of deities

Above: The geoglyph at Paracas, southern Peru, might have been a symbol of desert fertility and an orienteering aid to fishermen.

or supernatural beings who were believed to be responsible for bringing or withholding the rains.

Some lines may be related to astronomical observations – especially the positions of the sun through the year – that reflect times for planting and harvesting. Geometric patterns are ritual pathways, created and owned by groups within Nazca social organization for ceremonial processions. Ceremony, praying to the gods for the elements of life itself, is part of the 'mystery' of the lines. The axes of most lines run parallel to watercourses. Other lines are just as clearly the paths between settlements and the ceremonial centres themselves.

The number of lines, and their creation over a period of 700–800 years, overmarking each other in great profusion, shows that they were not conceived as a grand overall plan. The lines and figures appear to have been made by and for small groups – perhaps even individuals. Some may have been created for a single ceremony; others were used repeatedly. 'Solid' cleared areas might have been for congregations, while figures probably formed ritual pathways to be walked by people for specific ritual purposes.

CEQUE PATHWAYS

The *ceque* system of sacred routes was a uniquely Inca theoretical and practical concept interwoven with myth, astronomical observation, architectural alignment, and the social and geographical divisions of the empire. Sacred routes, however, were vital parts of pre-Inca cultures as well, and in this light the Inca *ceque* lines can be seen as integral with a long tradition of systems of sacred routes and pathways dating from pre-Hispanic Andean culture.

Ceques were straight, sacred 'lines' radiating from the Coricancha sacred precinct in Cuzco. Each line linked numerous *huacas* along its length. There were 41 such lines uniting 328 *huacas* and survey points within and around Cuzco. It is perhaps significant that the 328 *huacas* and stations correspond to

Below: Map showing the ceque *system of sacred or ritual routes linking the shrines and their locations.*

the number of days in the 12 sidereal lunar months (328/12 = the 27.3-day period of the rotation of the moon around the Earth–moon centre of mass). They were grouped according to 'upper' (*hanan*) and 'lower' (*hurin*) Cuzco and thus to the four quarters of the empire. Although theoretically straight, for practical purposes *ceques* sometimes had to obey the restrictions of the actual terrain through which they ran.

MULTIPLE PURPOSES

Points along the lines also served to regulate land holdings, water distribution, labour divisions, and ritual and ceremonial activities. *Ceques* were used as processional routes followed by *capacocha* (sacrificial individuals) at the beginnings of their journeys to the place of sacrifice. Combinations of *ceques* and their associated *huacas* distinguished the different *panaca* kin-group land-holdings within Inca society.

Above: Inca roads followed valley routes between cities, crossing mountain passes and river gorges using grass-fibre bridges.

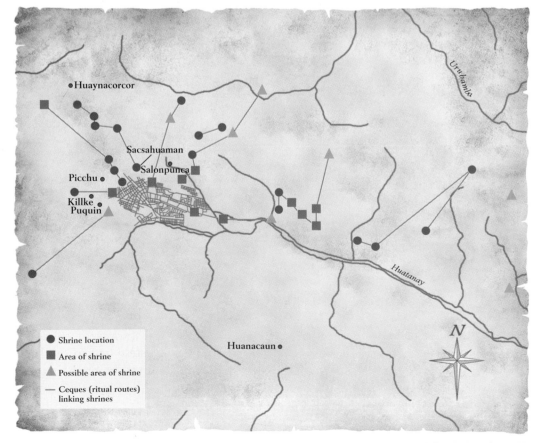

Shrine location
Area of shrine
Possible area of shrine
— Ceques (ritual routes) linking shrines

For example, sunset on 26 April and the observation of the setting of the Pleiades on or about 15 April were made from the same place in the Capac Usnu plaza in central Cuzco. The settings were viewed between two stone pillars, together regarded as a *huaca*, which had been erected on the skyline west of the city. Farther on, beyond the horizon, another *huaca* was the spring named Catachillay, another name for the Pleiades.

The movements of Mayu, the Milky Way, were linked to the *ceque* system by a division separating the four quarters along the intercardinal (between-the-compass-points) axis of Mayu, and the southernmost point of Mayu's movement in the night sky.

The 16th-century Spanish chronicler Juan de Betanzos describes the sixth *ceque* of Antisuyu quarter, on which lay the sixth *huaca*, as 'the house of the puma'. Here the mummified body of the wife of the emperor Pachacuti Inca Yupanqui was kept, to whom child sacrifices were offered.

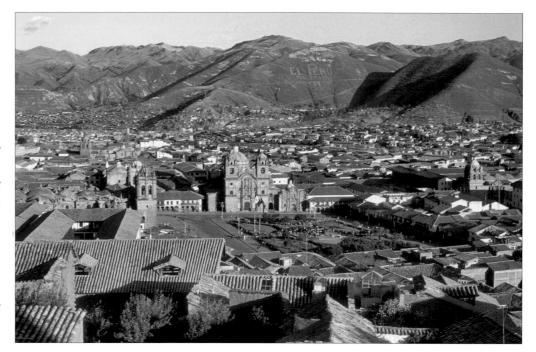

CEQUES AND SOCIAL STRUCTURE

Once again it was the vital importance of water in Andean life that formed an important part in the creation and use of the *ceque* ritual routes. The four *suyus* (quarters) of the Inca Empire, represented in the four divisions of Cuzco, were demarcated by the organization of the flow of water through the city. In turn, the radiating *ceque* lines organized the kinship *ayllu* groups into a hierarchy of positions either up or down river. This hierarchy itself reflected the nature of Inca society, in which different *ceque* lines were associated with the different bloodlines, particularly with the royal *panacas*, each of which was the origin of one of the primary descendants of the Inca ruler.

Thus, each *ceque* was created by and held information about irrigation, the Inca calendar and religious worship. Each *ceque* and its functions were maintained and tended by the appropriate kinship group

and social rank – aristocratic, mixed-blood or common – in a rotational system as the *ceque* lines were marked off around the horizon surrounding Cuzco.

In his *Historia del Nuevo Mundo*, Bernabé de Cobo describes the eighth *ceque* in the Chinchaysuyu (north-west quadrant). At its seventh *huaca*, a hill called Sucanca, a channel brought water from Chinchero. Two towers erected on the hill marked the position of the rising sun on the day when maize planting had to begin. Consequently, sacrifices at the *huaca* were directed to the sun, soliciting him to appear and shine through the towers at the appropriate time.

The system of *ceque* lines also regulated the Inca organization of annual labour, especially seasonal labour to do with agriculture and the maintenance of irrigation systems. Once a year, in the central plaza of upper (*hurin*) Cuzco, a ritual ploughing took place. Chosen representatives from 40 families selected from the four quarters dug up as if for planting a designated portion of the plaza field. Such a system of shared civic responsibilities and duties in prearranged patterns and rituals, and at determined times through the seasons of the year, appear to be a culmination of such systematic practices in pre-Inca cultures.

Left: The modern Inca Trail near Intipunku, Peru, follows the route of an ancient Inca road from Cuzco.

Above: The modern Plaza de Armas, Cuzco, was the ancient Huacaypata Plaza, centre of the Inca capital.

WHERE ARE THEY NOW?

The Dutch anthropologist Tom Zuidema devoted more than 40 years to the study of *ceques* and the sources of their organization and meaning. The *ceque* routes are described in considerable detail in Cobo's chronicle and other Inca colonial sources. However, the structures, such as towers at *huacas*, have long since been dismantled.

In the late 1970s Zuidema and archaeo-astronomer Anthony Aveni devoted four seasons of fieldwork to careful interpretations of the chronicles and surveyed the likely routes of *ceques* and locations of the *huacas* in Cobo's descriptions, using their knowledge of the terrain and landscape around Cuzco. Their efforts proved the validity of the system. In addition to mapping the locations of numerous *huacas*, they located three original places where astronomical *huacas* were used for measurements. One was a pair of towers to mark sunset at the June solstice, situated on a hill called Lacco, north of Cuzco. The second, another pair of towers, marked the December solstice from the Coricancha. The third was four pillars on Cerro Picchu, in western Cuzco, marking planting time; sighted from the *ushnu* stone in the Coricancha, they were used to track the sun on its mid-August passage through its lowest point.

CHAPTER FOUR

EARLY SETTLERS TO EMPIRE BUILDERS

The sweep of human history in the New World started at least 15,000 years ago, when humans migrated into the New World from the Old World, though the exact timing and detail of how long this journey took are obscured in the distant past.

During the Lithic, or Archaic, Period, humans began to live a more sedentary lifestyle. As with early human culture in the Old World, the existence and nature of the beliefs of these earliest South Americans can only be deduced from the very few facts available, combined with speculation.

In the earliest settlements, South Americans developed a more stable source of food in the beginnings of domestication of both plants and animals. Hunting and gathering and the exploitation of sea resources were never abandoned, however.

Later, the development of ceramics and, later still, metallurgy brought greater and greater divisions of labour within Andean societies, and consequently greater complexity. Sophisticated architecture, including U-shaped complexes, and masonry and adobe building techniques also developed.

Social hierarchies, elitism and rulership evolved alongside technological advances, as did religious belief and the explanation of human existence. In the absence of written records, archaeologists and historians seeking to understand the nature of the earliest Andean societies can only project what they know of later societies into the past.

Left: A marching, club-wielding warrior of the procession carved on stone monoliths at Cerro Sechín.

DEVELOPING COMMUNITIES

The Lithic Period did not end abruptly. An increasingly sedentary lifestyle developed towards the end of the period in some areas of South America, while in others a hunter-gatherer economy continued to form most or a significant part of people's lifestyles. In the Andean Area, village life became more important as an adaptation to developments in climate and habitat in the post-Ice Age environment. Sedentism, or the shift of people from living in non-permanent settlements to permanent settlements, was not at first accompanied by the development of pot-making in Andean South America, and so archaeologists call the period the Preceramic, or Formative, Period, or sometimes the Cotton Preceramic.

EARLY DOMESTICATION

Recognition of the usefulness of particular plants and animals fostered the special observation of these species and gradual greater attendance to their care and proliferation. The process of domestication was an evolutionary one, helped wittingly by humans but with practical rather than specific scientific understanding. In the archaeological record, the end result is recognizable only when genetic changes render the plants and animals biologically distinguishable from their wild progenitors. Thus, the beginning of the process cannot be pinpointed in time.

The results, however, show anatomical changes that are unmistakable. Equally, the regular cultivation of species in areas outside their normal wild distributions shows human mastery over their use. The earliest known domesticated plants date to about 10,000 years ago in the Andean Area, from Guitarrero Cave in northern Peru. Fibre plants dominate most assemblages of Lithic Period sites. Numerous wild hemp-like plants were used to make a wide range of artefacts, from tools and clothing to bedding. Many other kinds of plant were apparently of medicinal importance – and perhaps also of religious importance.

At Guitarrero Cave, locally native tubers, rhizomes, fruits, chillies and beans were found; from Tres Ventanas Cave, central Peru, at an altitude of 3,900m (12,800ft), also come tubers – ulluco and the potato; and from several cave deposits in the Ayacucho region come gourds.

THE FIRST CIVILIZATION?

As sedentary lifestyles increased from the time of these earliest domesticated plants to about 5,000 years ago, communities derived greater proportions of their nutrition from this source, alongside intensive tending and gathering of wild food sources. Andean Preceramic communities cultivated mostly self-watering regions, relying on rainfall and river run-off, and developed agro-pastoralism with llama herding. Coastal peoples pursued lifestyles exploiting the rich marine resources and cultivated cotton in seasonally watered valley bottoms. Such diversity was the beginning of the highland–lowland (or coastal) division.

The variety of environments within the Andean Area, both in different regions and at different heights, discouraged integration between communities, although it was forged within them. Nevertheless, the products of different regions were sought after and traded over long distances with increasing regularity, and with this trade the exchange of ideas was inevitable.

There is little evidence for powerful regional political leadership, but there *is* evidence of integrated communal effort in the form of the first monumental architecture between about 3000 and 2000BC. Inter-regional contact and trade also began the long Andean tradition of textile use – cotton cultivated in the lowlands and llama wool from herding in the highlands continued the earlier Andean Area focus on fibre technology, including the earliest weaving.

ARCHITECTURE AND TEXTILES

Increasing reliance on cultivation drew sierra populations to lower altitudes, into well-watered highland valleys and basins. Shared religious beliefs, manifested in architecture and on textiles, is known as

Left: The Preceramic Period adobe mud sculpture at the Temple of the Crossed Hands, at Kotosh (c.3000BC).

the Kotosh Religious Tradition in the highlands, after Kotosh, a site in highland central Peru at about 2,000m (6,600ft). Farther north, La Galgada was another highland valley community. Along the western coast more than a score of early sites are known, including Huaca Prieta, Salinas de Chao, Aspero and El Paraíso in north-central coastal Peru. Here architectural traditions called Supe, Aspero and El Paraíso developed.

The architecture at these sites varies in detail. For example, Supe Tradition communal structures are smaller and are associated with domestic buildings and artefacts, indicating they were constructed by their local communities. The much larger structures at sites of other traditions indicate more regional communal efforts, as centres for several communities. What is common, however, is the beginning of Andean central worship and a long generic tradition of ceremonial mounds and sunken courts or plazas. Both oval and rectangular examples

Below: Cotton, domesticated by at least 3000BC in the northern Peruvian coastal valleys, was a valuable commodity to trade.

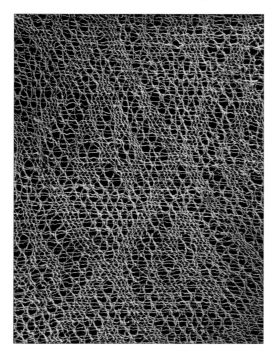

of sunken plazas are known. The two elements were made adjacent to each other and, in general, the plazas were smaller in area than the adjacent mounds.

These combined civic-ceremonial constructions are the earliest manifestations of Andean universal belief. They show both vertical and horizontal divisions of space for ceremonial purposes, and the special making and use of such space for communal worship drawing several communities together.

Alongside these architectural developments, textile design and decoration began to predominate among other media, such as stone, bone, shell, gourds, wood and basketry. Cotton was twined with spaced wefts and exposed warps; looping, knotting and simple weaving were also developed. The geometric nature of lattice-like fabric lent itself to

Above: Cotton was typically woven into open-work fabrics, such as this Chancay textile from the Late Intermediate Period.

angular decoration in different colours and to symmetry. Stripes, diamonds, squares and chevrons were used individually, in patterns, and to depict humanlike beings and animals that were important locally in an economic sense and universally as revered beings. Crabs, fish, raptors and serpents predominate.

Although the specifics of belief systems of such an early period can only be surmised, such detailed imagery, through its universality and repetition, reveals underlying religious belief. Coastal animals and motifs were copied in the highland traditions and vice versa. It seems that religion was, even at this early period, at the foundations of Andean civilization.

SOUTHERN CULTS: PARACAS AND PUKARÁ

Environmental decline occurred in the southern Andean Area, along the coast and in the Altiplano in the late Initial Period. In the Peruvian southern coastal desert, the natural aridity, exacerbated by drought in the inland mountains, presented a considerable challenge to the ingenuity of the coastal fishing village inhabitants. In the Titicaca Basin, the lake level fell dramatically and fields were abandoned all along the southern shores, as farmers could no longer raise crops or feed animals there.

PARACAS MUMMY BURIALS

The Paracas Peninsula was the site of a necropolis of elite burials. Apart from the Chinchorros mummy burials in northern Chile, the Paracas desiccated mummies are the earliest in the Andean Area, beginning a long tradition of mummification in Andean civilization. The elaborately wrapped, multilayered burial bundles demonstrate a preoccupation with the continued life, or participation in the present, of physically deceased important individuals. The richest ceramic and textile products, and exotic goods from afar, were saved for the burials; indeed, some goods were produced specifically for this purpose. Their existence begins the equally long Andean tradition of ancestor worship.

While the peninsula is the site of the Cavernas cemetery, the inhabitants who created it lived in the adjacent area inland around Cerro Colorado, where some 54ha (137 acres) of scattered domestic architecture has been found. The economy was based on local fishing.

The cemetery was a specially dedicated site. The dead were placed in their mummy bundles into large subterranean crypts, which were either bell-shaped pits or masonry-lined rectangular mausoleums. These were used through several generations, and the individuals appear to be kin. As the numbers of burials appear to exceed the requirements of the immediate adjacent settlements, it is

Above: The flying Oculate Being of the Paracas and Nazca southern coastal cultures, depicted on a woollen burial shroud.

thought that the necropolis was also a pilgrimage or cult centre serving communities through a wider region.

The stages for the preparation for these burials were inland in the Chincha Valley. These comprised low rectangular mounds aligned at the front and back of a high-walled central court, sunk to near ground level, such as the one found at Huaca Soto. The court walls are so thick that the complex is reminiscent of a single mound with a sunken summit courtyard. Huaca Soto comprised two interior courts, plus a thick-walled frontal entry court. The whole structure was 70m (230ft) by 200m (650ft) and stood 15m (49) high.

IMPORTANCE OF PUKARÁ

In the Altiplano around Lake Titicaca, emphasis on mother earth (Pacha Mama) and father sky (Yama Mama) continued as people remained close to the land and struggled to cope with drought. The importance of the regional centre at Chiripa waned and the site was eventually left to decline. The replacement for Chiripa as the focus of religion became the ceremonial centre of Pukará, some 75km (47 miles) north-west of the lake. Pukará arose around 400BC and exerted its influence over the Titicaca Basin for four centuries.

Unlike U-shaped complexes, Pukará comprised monumental masonry-clad structures terraced against the hillside. The principal terrace had a monumental staircase and was topped by a rectangular sunken court with one-room buildings around three sides, reminiscent of the Chiripa complex.

The hallmark of Pukará cult symbolic art was the depiction of *yaya* (male) and *mama* (female) figures on opposite sides of slab monoliths erected at Pukará and other sites. Other Pukará stone carving, pottery and textiles displayed ubiquitous Andean images, including felines, serpents, lizards and fish.

Like the Chavín Cult, Pukará art images featured disembodied human heads. Some of these were trophy heads accompanying realistically depicted humans; others accompanied supernatural beings with feline or serpentine attributes, as in the Chavín Cult, and are thought to represent shamans in transformational states. Many Pukará temple sites were rebuilt and used over several centuries. The assemblages of structures around Pukará sunken courts show considerable variety.

Above: Nested geometric patterns in the Pukará culture included the multi-stepped 'Andean Cross'.

In this way, Paracas, Pukará and Chavín styles, although distinct, show themselves to have a pan-Andean combination of features, including, especially, the Chavín emphasis on feline, serpentine and raptor attributes. The combination of cotton textiles and the importation of alpaca and llama wool for use by Paracas weavers shows another highland influence.

THE OCULATE BEING

One supernatural being or deity that stands out as distinctly Paracas, and which carries on in the succeeding Nazca civilization, is known as the Oculate Being. Depicted on textiles, the being was portrayed horizontally – as if flying upside-down – as if looking down on humankind, and crouching. His/her frontal face has characteristic large, circular, staring eyes, and long, streaming appendages originate from various parts of the body and end in trophy heads or small figures.

Below: Early Horizon Paracas mummified bodies were buried in multiple layers of cloth, the richness of which reflected their status.

Below: The bodies of Paracas mummies were tightly constricted into compact bundles and held by cords.

PARACAS AND PUKARÁ LINKS

There are generic artistic links between the Paracas and Pukará art styles and symbols used. Both styles feature monochrome and polychrome pottery with multicoloured motifs framed with incised lines. Some of the earliest phase styles, especially at Paracas, are attributed to Chavín influence because they represent a change from the local pottery that preceded it. There is an emphasis on non-human faces adorned with fangs and feline whiskers, especially on pottery. As Paracas pottery developed, it showed a more naturalistic style akin to Pukará ceramics. Local coastal subjects such as falcons, swallows, owls and foxes later predominated. The images and patterns painted on Paracas pottery were also used in their textiles.

PEOPLES OF THE EMPIRE

Spanish administrative and judicial archives contain chronicles and records of the Inca conquest of numerous ethnic groups, chiefdoms and political units called *señorios*. From these sources we have a veritable roster of the peoples of the empire.

RIVALS OF THE INCAS
Guaman Poma de Ayala's history refers to the chiefdom of the Ayarmacas, one of the many politico-ethnic divisions of the Acamama region around Cuzco. As the first powerful Inca rivals, the Ayarmacas played an instrumental role in the founding of Cuzco. Poma de Ayala identifies 'some first Incas' called Tocay Capac and Pinahua Capac, whom other sources call 'kings', or identify as generic

Below: One of the greatest Inca conquests involved capturing the Chimú fortresses, such as that of coastal Paramonga.

titles for the rulers of two allied chiefdoms – Ayarmaca and Pinahua – comprising 18 towns south of Cuzco.

Prolonged Ayarmaca campaigns against the Incas of Cuzco resulted in stalemate. However, as the Incas subdued other neighbours and expanded within the valley, the Ayarmaca lords were relegated to the status of local chiefs within the Inca hierarchy. As the Incas wrestled for control, their new arch-rivals became the Chancas, whose defeat in 1438 was a defining point in the rise of the Inca state, and the traditional date for the beginning of the empire, along with Pachacuti Inca Yupanqui's ascent to the throne.

PEOPLES OF THE INCA EMPIRE
Pachacuti turned his attention to the Altiplano chiefdoms. His predecessor Viracocha had formed an alliance with the Lupaqas of Chucuito against the Hatun Colla, but

Above: Huayna Capac, 12th of the Inca dynasty and the last great conquering emperor, ruled from 1493 until 1526.

success against the Chancas changed Pachacuti's perspective on domination. The Collas were utterly defeated in battle, and the peace scene frequently depicted on *kero* drinking vessels shows the Collas wearing especially tall headdresses, emphasizing the cultural variety and distinction between ethnic groups. At the victory celebration in Cuzco, Pachacuti ordered the beheading of the Colla leaders, warning others who might resist.

The effect was immediate and the remaining Altiplano lords accepted Inca overlordship without further resistance. This Cuntisuyu quarter formed the core of the empire, incorporating the chiefdoms of the Soras, Lucanas, Andahuaylas, Canas, Canchis, Paucarcollas, Pacajes and Azángaros, and exposing the western coastal *señorio* of Collao.

The Chinchas of Collao submitted peacefully at the intimidating approach of Inca armies led by Tupac Yupanqui. Pachacuti and Tupac next expanded north, creating Chinchaysuyu quarter, valley chiefdoms falling one after another: the

Below: In less than 100 years, the Incas subdued peoples from Ecuador to Chile and from the Pacific to the Amazon Rainforest.

Guarco and Lunahuaná chiefdoms in the central Andes; the Collec *señorio*, including the Chuquitanta, Carabayllo, Zapan, Macas, Guaraui, Guancayo and Quivi chiefdoms; and the Ychsma *señorio*.

THE KINGDOM OF THE CHIMÚ

The Inca armies marched on the vast, ancient northern Kingdom of Chimú. Garcilasco de la Vega's *Comentarios Reales de los Incas* describes the confrontation:

The brave Chimú [Minchançaman], his arrogance and pride now tamed, appeared before the prince [Tupac Inca Yupanqui] with as much submission and humility, and grovelled on the ground before him, worshipping him and repeating the same request [for pardon] as he had made through his ambassadors. The prince received him affectionately in order to relieve [his] grief … [and] bade two of the captains raise him from the ground. After hearing him, [Tupac] told him that all that was past was forgiven. … The Inca had not come to deprive him of his estates and authority, but to improve his idolatrous religion, his laws, and his customs.

Unlike the treatment of Colla leaders, Tupac set a new precedent, incorporating new states and recognizing their integrity under Inca overlordship. Perhaps the size and importance of Chimú prompted special treatment.

Farther north, the coastal chiefdoms of the Quito, Cañaris, Huancavilcas, Manta and Puná were conquered; then the Huarochirí, Yauyos, and the *señorio* of Guzmango. These northern chiefdoms fell so rapidly that there was hardly time

Above: The centre of the empire was Cuzco, here seen from the fortress-temple of Sacsahuaman overlooking the city.

for incorporation and consolidation; archaeology and the chronicles, however, attest to the rapid imposition of Inca rule, installation of local elites as provincial governors and collection of tax produce into large centres for redistribution.

OUTSIDERS AND REBELS

The Incas also recognized peoples beyond imperial borders, against whom their campaigns were less successful. The chronicles of Tupac Yupanqui's incursions into the selva of Antisuyu quarter mention the Opataris, Manosuyu, Mañaris, Yanaximes, Chunchos and Paititi.

Many chiefdoms accepted diminution of their authority reluctantly. Tupac's son Huayna Capac campaigned against the Chiriguanas of Collasuyu quarter, and, in the far north, the Chachapoyas of Chinchaysuyu, the Caranquis, Otavalos, Cayambis, Cochasquis and Pifos, all of whom had rebelled. The Huanca of Chinchaysuyu allied themselves to Pizarro in a final bid to throw off Inca domination.

The Incas strove for political unity by utilizing local rulers and incorporating them into the Inca hierarchy, giving local elites and subjects a sense of belonging. Nevertheless, local independence had lasted for generations, so there was considerable resentment of Inca impositions, particularly among more far-flung peoples. This potential instability, especially at the death of Huayna Capac in 1526, played into Spanish hands.

CHAPTER SIX

POWER AND WARFARE

By the end of the Initial Period, civilization in the Andean Area had established an underlying unity in religious concepts and some basic civic-ceremonial architectural forms, culminating in the cohesion in the Chavín Cult in the Early Horizon. Subsequent periods continued the alternation of less-unified periods and more politically unified horizons, although in every period there were some kingdoms or empires.

Patterns established in earlier periods continued to focus on three areas: the central and northern Peruvian coastal valleys, the central and southern Peruvian/Bolivian sierras and Altiplano, and the southern Peruvian and northern Chilean coastal deserts. Within each of these areas powerful social hierarchies developed and elite individuals ruled alongside a specialized priesthood or state shamans. Elite individuals were buried elaborately in rich tombs, sumptuously adorned and often accompanied by sacrificial victims. State cults of the dead flourished, establishing the principle of a continuously revolving cycle of life and death and the perpetuation of the dead in the living world.

The principles of state control over ordinary citizens became stronger and more elaborate, culminating in one of the two greatest empires ever established in the Americas: the Inca Empire. The chronicles and histories preserved by Spanish priests and administrators, together with archaeological discoveries, make it possible to gain a detailed picture of the way of life and beliefs of the Incas.

Left: This painted Chimú textile depicts a shaman in a trance, surrounded by snarling felines, serpents and birds.

THE WARI EMPIRE

Huari was the capital city of the Wari Empire and the northern rival of Tiwanaku. Together the two empires represent the political cohesion that united the Middle Horizon for more than 500 years.

BIRTH OF AN IMPERIAL STATE

Wari dominated the central Andes and coastal valleys, and expanded into the regions of the north almost to the Ecuadorian border. One of its northern-most outposts was the city of Cajamarca in northern Peru; its southernmost was Pikillaqta near Cuzco. It met Tiwanaku expansion at the Pass of La Raya, south of Cuzco, and openly confronted Tiwanaku in the upper reaches of the Moquegua drainage area west of Titicaca, where it established a colony on the defensive summit of Cerro Baúl. This region, split between Tiwanaku in the north-west and Wari in the south-east, constituted a buffer zone between the two empires.

Below: The need for the hilltop fortress of Carangas is an example of the tense rivalry between the Wari and Tiwanaku empires.

From humble beginnings in the 3rd century AD, major constructions at Huari from the 5th century reflect the city's growing power. Its main period of imperial expansion lasted from about AD600 to 800.

The capital occupied the plateau of a mountain valley at about 2,800m (9,180ft) above sea level between the Huamanga and Huanta basins. Serving as a civic, residential and religious centre, it grew rapidly to cover more than 100ha (247 acres), then 200ha (495 acres), then 300ha (740 acres), with an additional periphery of residential suburbs occupying a further 250ha (620 acres). Its population has been variously estimated at 10,000–35,000 inhabitants.

From about 600 the Wari state spread a dominant religion, characterized by a distinctive symbolic art, through military expansion in much the same way that its coastal rival, the Moche, had expanded earlier in the northern coastal region.

Shortly before 800 there appears to have been a political crisis that caused building within the capital to slacken and cease. Simultaneously, the political

Above: The city of Huari was gradually expanded through regular additions of angular walled precincts and dressed-stone sectors.

centre and religious shrine of Pachacamac, on the central Peruvian coast, began to reassert itself and possibly even to rival Wari power. Pachacamac had flourished since later Early Intermediate Period times and had only recently been occupied by the Wari. Similarly, in its north-west provinces, the rising local power of the Sicán lords of the Lambayeque Valley challenged Wari overlordship in the late 7th century. Wari expansion ended abruptly and the capital was abandoned by AD800.

RUINS OF THE CAPITAL

The architecture of the site of Huari, although megalithic, has not survived well. Some of it approximates the grandeur of the ceremonial architecture at Tiwanaku, although more crudely. Numerous walls remain as high as

Above: The rigidly planned border fortress of Pikillaqta, the southernmost Wari town, included an extensive defensive wall.

6–12m (20–40ft). There were several rectangular compounds, and some buildings had projecting walls that supported multiple storeys.

In contrast to Tiwanaku, however, Huari's rapid expansion appears to have occurred at random, without the deliberate and preconceived planning of its competitor. The huge enclosure of Cheqo Wasi (or Huasi) included dressed stone-slab chambers. Two important temple complexes were Vegachayoq Moqo and Moraduchayoq, the latter a semi-subterranean compound resembling the one at Tiwanaku. In keeping with the comparatively frenetic pace of Huari's development, the Moraduchayoq Temple was dismantled around AD650.

SHARED RELIGION

Wari and Tiwanaku's political ambitions and military aims made them political rivals, yet they also shared symbolic religious imagery and mythology.

Much of the religious and mythological art imagery of Tiwanaku and Wari was virtually identical, which demonstrates religious continuity from the Early Horizon through the Early Intermediate Period. Despite military opposition, scholars entertain the possibility that religious missionaries from one city visited the other. It might have been that the priests were willing to set politics aside and let religious beliefs transcend such matters.

Continuity and similarities of religious symbols used in art include, in particular, the Staff Deity image, but also winged and running falcon- and condor-headed creatures – often wielding clubs – and severed trophy heads. It is reasoned that similarities in imagery show similarities in religious and cosmological belief. It seems that the gods of Chavín endured as the Staff Deity of Tiwanaku and Wari, and were responsible for human origins and for the fertility of crops and flocks. Winged beings appear both accompanying the Staff Deity and independently, and were depicted running, floating, flying or kneeling. The Staff Deity – with mask-like face, radiating head rays (sometimes ending in serpent heads), and tunic, belt and kilt – appears on pottery and architecture and might have been the prototype for the creator god Viracocha.

Despite such apparent religious unity, the focus of religious imagery in Wari differed from that in Tiwanaku. In Wari it was applied primarily to portable objects, particularly to ceramics; in Tiwanaku, however, it was concentrated on monumental stone architecture, and appeared less frequently on pottery or textiles. Thus, while Wari ceramics and textiles spread the word far and wide, Tiawanaku imagery was more confined to standing monuments at the capital and a few other sites. The ceremonial core at Tiwanaku was designed and developed as a preconceived plan, and was therefore one of public ceremony and, apparently, participation. The Wari capital of Huari, by contrast, appears to have developed more haphazardly, and religious structures were smaller and more private, implying that they were the focus of ritual of a more personal and intimate nature.

RIVALS OR ALLIES?

Given these similarities and differences, the exact nature of the relationship between the two kingdoms or empires remains enigmatic. The two empires seemed to keep each other at arms' length, but they may have exchanged political and religious ambassadors to each other's capital city. Nevertheless, it is clear that religious concepts and imagery prevailed through the politically fragmented Early Intermediate Period as well as within the more unified imperial Middle Horizon.

Below: Although political rivals, Wari and Tiwanaku shared a religion, here represented by a kero *drinking cup with a serpentine motif.*

PART TWO

MYTH AND RELIGION

The peoples of the ancient Andean civilizations regarded their entire surroundings as sacred. Maintaining a balanced relationship with the landscape, seascape and skyscape was considered essential to their well-being in the land of the living. Shamans were responsible for maintaining a dialogue with the past and, theoretically, with things to come in an endless cycle of history. Sacred powers were everywhere, and were both revered and feared. Ritual offerings, sacrifices and the maintenance of a link between the living and the dead were a necessary part of everyday life. Although we call it 'myth' today, Andean peoples' beliefs and their perception of the universe was their religion.

This part of the book concentrates on the deities and their stories as recorded mostly by Spanish chroniclers and by native record-keepers who were converted by Spanish priests. Although there were elements of regionalism, many deities were universally accepted throughout the Andean Area, sometimes under different names. Ancient Andean beliefs tended to be widespread, both at a given time and through time. The narrative of Andean belief in a cyclical history even incorporated their eventual defeat by outsiders, but continues today in the belief that time will turn again, reversing their defeat in perpetual revolution.

The Paracas–Nazca Oculate Being is shown flying across the sky on this woollen burial shroud.

CHAPTER SEVEN

A PANTHEON OF GODS

Sanctity permeated the ancient Andean world. Sacred powers were everywhere, in all living things. Survival in this world, the land of the living, was dependent not only on producing enough to eat, but also on revering the gods and appeasing them through rituals, sacrifices and offerings. At the same time, there was a fatalism in the belief in the great cycle of being, of life and death, which gave rise to the reverence of ancestors.

The peoples of the Andean Area held a range of beliefs and appear to have worshipped a pantheon of deities with control over different aspects of nature. Their religious beliefs developed from the earliest times, and they can be detected in the architecture and art of the earliest Andean civilizations. Many deities were universally accepted throughout the Andean Area, sometimes called by different names but having the same essential attributes, powers and roles.

A linking factor throughout Andean life was that of continuity, of how all things are connected and so part of a cycle, and this was demonstrated through the concepts of mutual exchange, duality and collectivity, which were all vital parts of spiritual and daily life for ancient Andeans. Continuity was intensely developed in Andean civilization through the pilgrimage centres, such as Chavín de Huántar and Pachacamac, that persisted over centuries and endured despite political rivalry and changing political developments.

Left: The central figure of the Gateway of the Sun, at Tiwanaku, is a ray-encircled face in the pose of the Chavín Staff Deity.

THEMES AND BELIEFS

The long sequence of development among Andean highland and lowland peoples fostered mutually beneficial relationships between cultures. Constant contact between regions brought the exchange of ideas as well as produce and commodities.

ANDEAN THEMES

Through Andean history, common themes were expressed in art and architecture. Coastal animals and motifs were copied in highland traditions and vice versa.

The early combination of temple platforms and sunken courts shows this exchange of ideas in the architectural elements of the ceremonial centre. Platforms mimic mountain peaks and plateaux, while sunken courts mimic valleys and coastal desert oases. It can be argued that ritual progression through such ceremonial complexes reflects the symbiotic relationship between highland

Below: Part of the outcrop of the sacred Inca huaca at Qenqo, north of Cuzco, was believed to be a giant seated puma turned to stone.

Right: An Early Intermediate Period Nazca bridge-spouted pot depicts the Oculate Being accompanied by trophy heads.

and lowland cultures and between mountain and coastal deities.

This architectural combination also shows the early appearance of the Andean concept of duality. The late Preceramic Period union of platform mound and sunken court, both in highland and lowland sites, constituted the first widespread Andean 'religion'. To agricultural peoples, the sunken court was probably the focus for the worship of 'mother earth' – for the ritual re-enactment of birth or creation represented by spring crops. The ascent of the platform may have been the recognition of the upper world in which the god of creation dwelled, or from which came the waters that made agriculture possible.

The highland site of Chavín de Huántar not only combined the elements of platform and sunken court, but also introduced the idea of a sacred location widely accepted as the focus of worship for peoples throughout the central Andes and coast. The Chavín Cult developed the labyrinthine temple complex within which cult statuary was secreted, with all its obscure meaning, perhaps interpretable only by shamans.

With the development of the Chavín cult also came religious art expressing duality and a prototype supreme creator god, forerunner to representations of Viracocha in later Andean civilizations. The Staff Deity, significantly represented both as male and female, was an undisguised representation of duality. In varying forms, a deity holding staffs with outstretched arms was an artistic motif from Chavín to Inca times. In the courtyard of Chavín de Huántar's New Temple stood the 0.5m (1½ft) stone sculpture of the supreme deity. Holding a *Strombus* shell in one hand and a *Spondylus* shell in the other, the deity also manifested duality, as a metaphor for the balancing of male and female forces in the universe, and the union of opposing forces, providing completion through unity.

COMMON BELIEFS

Thus, despite variations in regional and cultural detail, the earliest ceremonial centres reflect common elements of belief.

The continuing highland–lowland interchange was cemented in the recognition of certain ceremonial centres as places of pilgrimage, Chavín de Huántar being the first. Platforms with sunken courtyards and pilgrimage centres were elements of Andean civilization for 2,500 years. Pilgrimage centres were recognized by both highland and coastal states, linking regions and persisting through political change. The cult centre of Chavín de Huántar endured for more than 500 years, while the site and oracle of coastal Pachacamac, beginning in the 1st century AD, lasted more than a millennium.

The Incas had a complex calendar of worship based on the movements of heavenly bodies, including solar solstices

Above: An Early Intermediate Period Nazca sheet-gold burial mask. A burial with such a mask indicates high-status.

Below: A Late Intermediate Period Chimú mummy bundle with a copper burial mask, painted red, feather headdress and two flutes.

and equinoxes, lunar phases, the synodic cycle of Venus, the rising and setting of the Pleiades, the rotational inclinations of the Milky Way, and the presence within the Milky Way of 'dark cloud constellations' (stellar voids). Consultation of auguries concerning these movements was vital at momentous times of the year, such as planting time, harvest time and the beginning of the ocean fishing season. Inca practices represent the final stage of the development of such beliefs.

Sacrifice, both human and animal, and a variety of offerings were common. Ritual strangulation and beheading are well attested in burials and art such as ceramic painting, murals, architectural sculpture, textiles and metalwork.

As well as pilgrimage sites, tens of thousands of places – *huacas* – were held sacred. Like pilgrimage centres, their importance could endure for centuries. *Huacas* could be springs (emphasizing the importance of water), caves (prominent in human origin mythology), mountains, rocks or stones, fields or towns where important events had taken place, lakes or islands in them, or man-made objects

such as stone pillars erected at specific locations.

Shrines and temples were sometimes built at *huacas*, but just as often the object/place was left in its natural state.

The ritual use of hallucinogenic drugs was widespread. Coca (*Erythroxylon coca*) leaves were chewed in a complex and multi-stage ritual connected with war and sacrifice. Cactus buds and hallucinogenic mushrooms were also used.

The reverence for ancestors is evident in the special treatment of mummified burials in the Chinchorros culture of northern coastal Chile. Such practice developed into ancestor worship and became charged with special ritual, governed by the cyclical calendar by Inca times. Mummified remains of ancestors were carefully kept in special buildings, rooms or chambers, or in caves, and were themselves considered *huacas*. They were brought out on ritual occasions to participate in the festivals and to be offered delicacies of food and drink, as well as objects and prayers.

Preoccupation with death included the underworld. Skeletal figures, depictions of priests imitating the dead to visit the underworld, and skeletal figures with sexual organs or the dead embracing women were associated with fertility beliefs and the source of life in the underworld.

PACHACUTI – THE ENDLESS CYCLE

To the ancient Andeans everything around them, in all directions, was sacred. They believed themselves to be in a universe that was forever in cycle, *pachacuti*, in an endless revolution of time and history. The concept of *pachacuti* is further revealed in the Andean belief that humankind went through several phases of creation, destruction and re-creation. This progression was held to reflect the gods' desire to create an increasingly perfected form of humans. Honour and worship of the gods was so important that it took several efforts to create beings of proper humility. This veneration was essential because it was 'known' that at the slightest provocation they were capable of destroying the world.

A DIVIDED UNIVERSE

The ancient Andeans' universe comprised three levels: the world of the living, which the Incas called Kai Pacha, the world below, called Uku Pacha, and the world of the heavens, called Hanan Pacha. Kai Pacha comprised the relatively flat surface of the earth and lay between the other two. As the world of humans, Kai Pacha was also called Hurin Pacha – lower world. As well as this vertical arrangement, the

Inca universe was divided by two horizontal axes running through the points of the compass. The centre of both realms ran through Cuzco, where the vertical axis of the three realms and the horizontal axes intersected.

Pervading the entire universe was the creator god – the all-powerful, "formless" one – Viracocha (as the Inca and many others knew him).

Above: Warrior figures on this Paracas burial textile, c.500BC, are shown in the symbolic pose of the Chavín Staff Deity.

AN ECOLOGICAL RELATIONSHIP

The relationship maintained between ancient Andeans and their universe can be characterized as 'ecological'. Because they perceived their environment as sacred, they believed that they were on earth not to exploit it but rather to enjoy its benefits through the grace of the gods. The relationship was one of deity power and human supplication. Humans considered themselves to be not the centre or focus of the world but only one group among all living things – including animals, plants and the stars. Thus humans appealed to the gods for their permission to make use of the various other elements of the world. Indeed, the animals, plants and stars were rather more important than humans, for it was in them that the gods were personified.

Left: Long-distance trade contacts also spread imagery. Here a rainforest monkey decorates a coastal desert Nazca ceramic vessel.

Right: An Inca textile showing a deity or a shaman, impersonating a god with sky-snake image and the stance of the Staff Deity.

AN EVOLVING RELIGION

More is known about Inca beliefs than other beliefs of the Andean Area because they were formed into an official state religion and cult of the emperor, Inti, as the earthly representative of the sun. Inca religion itself was the final stage in a long sequence of development from primitive beliefs. Inca conquest brought their people into contact with many other cultures and regions, each of which also had its own religious development.

Upon conquest, Spanish clergy and administrators recorded Inca beliefs and concepts in their attempts to understand more about the peoples of the empire. Archaeologists believed that the concepts and physical remains of Inca religion can be projected into the pre-Inca past. They also detect many common themes in ancient Andean development because the archaeological evidence indicates that pre-Inca deities, whose names are mostly unknown, nevertheless represented the same or very similar concepts to those of Inca deities.

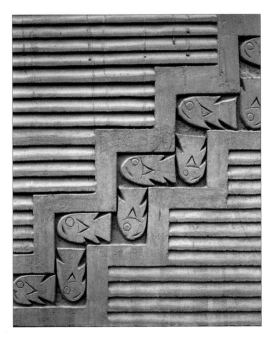

FUNDAMENTAL DUALITY

Following the fundamental Andean belief in duality, the universe and everything in it comprised two parts in opposition, but striving for completion through unity, thus male/female, light/dark, hot/cold, good/evil, the sun/the moon.

To civilizations based primarily on agriculture for their day-to-day existence, the natural world and its physical forces represented essential elements of survival. The natural elements were considered divine and ruled human existence as evidence of the gods' powers. Ancient Andeans naturally sought to give the

Left: Fish, perhaps in a river channel, decorate the sculpted compound mud walls at the Chimú capital of Chan Chan.

deities and their powers 'forms' in representational art and architecture, and common themes can be detected from at least the Initial Period in its ceremonial architecture. A pantheon of deities and beliefs is evident from at least Chavín times in the Early Horizon.

The Andean pantheon in its entirety was extremely complex and varied throughout the regions. Almost universal, however, was the belief in a creator god, known as Viracocha in the highland and inland regions and Pachacmac among Pacific coastal cultures. In addition, the sun and the moon were deities called by numerous names in different cultures and through time. Usually, but not always, the sun was regarded as male and the moon as female.

COLLECTIVE THINKING

Reciprocity within society was complemented by another concept, collectivity, which permeated life at all levels.

A COLLECTIVE SOCIETY

Collectivity was the overriding mode of operation in Inca (and their predecessors') society. Corporate thinking demanded that the group always took precedence over the individual, since the individual was part of the whole and could not function effectively except as part of the whole. Collectivity complements reciprocity in the idea that all things are connected and therefore part of a whole and of the cycle of the universe. As a supreme example, the Inca Inti shows reciprocity and collectivity at the same time. As the earthly representative of Inti the sun, he was an intermediary between the people and the gods – and thus part of the collectivity that was necessary for the whole to function effectively. In contradiction of this, however, he was individual and supreme above all other Incas.

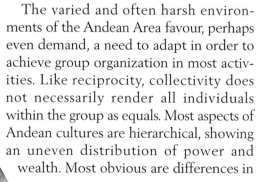

The varied and often harsh environments of the Andean Area favour, perhaps even demand, a need to adapt in order to achieve group organization in most activities. Like reciprocity, collectivity does not necessarily render all individuals within the group as equals. Most aspects of Andean cultures are hierarchical, showing an uneven distribution of power and wealth. Most obvious are differences in

Above: A less elaborate burial textile from Nazca shows a stylized human figure within a simple, repetitive pattern.

burials, from royal and rich elite tombs to common graves, and from elaborate 'natural' interment to ritual sacrifice.

The concept can be traced to the earliest Andean civilizations. Architecture, from these times, demonstrates such hierarchy in quality of construction, decoration and apparent function. Common dwellings surrounded great ceremonial centres that were the hubs of the cities. Such architecture, however, represents the ultimate in corporate thinking in the marshalling and command of the labour to build ceremonial structures to serve the community. The Incas

Left: A mass-produced Inca chicha *jug and* kero *drinking cup represent state-controlled industry and the redistribution of goods.*

Above: The Incas collected agricultural produce into state-controlled warehouses for redistribution according to need and rank.

ingeniously incorporated subject peoples into the empire, embracing myriad cultures and nuances of belief and local political, social and economic arrangements. Yet, they also represent the extreme of inequality within collectivity – the few ruling the many in the pyramid of power; the Incas, who numbered about 100,000, ruled more than ten million people.

The social fission that might result from challenging environments and from such inequality was mediated by ritual, to re-emphasize social collectivity or corporateness. The Inca Quechua term for such ritual was *tinku*, referring to the joining of two to form one.

THE IMPORTANCE OF ROLE

Andean artistic collectivity is shown by a general sparsity of portraiture, historical detail and narrative. The details of special features, physical location or the actions of specific people are usually unimportant: it is the person's role that is important to show, and religious art overridingly features supernatural imagery. The deities have aspects by which they can be recognized, and it is these aspects that must be shown accurately. Artistic decoration emphasizes continuous and repetitious patterning, itself an obvious manifestation of 'corporateness'. As early as the Initial Period, the architectural monolithic mosaic at Cerro Sechín shows this concept, forming converging processions of figures and banners. Rather than representing individuals, the figures are stylized representations of warriors and captives in a procession of conquest, triumph and sacrifice – a *tinku* ritual and convergence of duality in ceremonial temple architecture.

Moche art is a notable exception to these concepts. Recent research and discoveries show portraiture and narrative, especially in Moche ceramics and in the scenes painted on them, and historical details, in which the entombed in elite burials represent the deities or priests and priestesses depicted on pots and murals.

ARTISTIC ANONYMITY

The extensive use of moulds in ceramic production and repetitious dual- and mirror-imagery also show collectivity. Although the names of individual artists are unknown, scholars recognize their particular styles. The distinctive 'makers' marks' on the millions of adobe bricks used in the construction of the pyramid platforms of the Moche capital are another demonstration of corporate thinking. The idea was not to distinguish the brick-makers but rather to account for the labour or quota required of collective work units.

Right: Llama effigy figures. Llama herding for wool and other products was also state-controlled.

The seemingly intentional anonymity of ancient Andean artists, craftsmen and labourers does not render their art generic. Individual sculptures, pots, murals and metalwork are idiosyncratic, dynamic and distinctive. They can be recognized by archaeologists today and therefore must have been identifiable when made. The specific styles of ancient Andean cultures and regions are certainly distinctive. However, within these there are styles of imagery, some of which lasted for more than 1,000 years, even though some details changed over time.

Nevertheless, it is the image and concept of a piece that are important, not its maker. The religious message was paramount, and that subsumed the whole. This combination of collectivity and stressing the abstract in art rendered ancient Andean culture highly sophisticated yet unconcerned with specific or individual conspicuousness or eminence.

CHAPTER EIGHT

HONOURING THE GODS

In his *Historia del Nuevo Mundo*, the 17th-century Spanish chronicler and historian Father Bernabe Cobo names 317 different shrines in Inca Cuzco alone. From this, there is no doubt that religion permeated Inca society.

From the earliest times, it is evident that ancient Andean cultures honoured their gods. The treatment shown in special burials and in the construction of special architecture in the midst of domestic dwellings in towns and cities reveals a deep reverence for things beyond day-to-day survival. Whatever their nature, religious considerations were intermixed.

Political arrangements came and went. Rulers were seen to participate in religious ritual, and to be representatives of the gods on Earth. Yet when kingdoms fell and regions were broken up into smaller political entities, the gods remained. In this sense, religion was both integral to and independent of politics in ancient Andean civilization.

The gods and goddesses were depicted on all media: ceramics, textiles and metalwork, and on small and monumental stone, clay and wooden sculpture. They were both portrayed directly, as men and women dressed to represent them, and symbolized in architectural complexes. Features of the landscape were held to be imbued with their presence and therefore representative of them.

Left: Supernatural beings, including a figure reminiscent of the Staff Deity, on a Moche dyed and finely woven cotton textile.

PILGRIMAGE AND ORACLE SITES

The difficulties inherent in explaining supernatural concepts through images difficult to produce with the existing technology may have fostered the growth of pilgrimage centres. Their symbolic art, meant to show the complexities of supernatural belief, could be combined with complex architecture and mystery in a central place. The spread of religious ideas could be accomplished by bringing converts to a place held most sacred and then dispersing them again, convinced of or reinforced in their belief in the cult. Portable art decorated with the symbolic images of the religious concepts would help remind those living at distance from the cult centre of the tenets of the cult.

Similarly, the sacredness of a cult centre, where the truth was held and expounded by its priests, would become a focus for other-worldly experience. The architecture of the centre could provoke and enhance such an experience.

Below: The Semi-subterranean Court enclosed formal ritual space at Tiwanaku, capital city of the Titicaca Basin.

A WESTERN VIEW?
These general concepts seem self-evident, yet they are overlain with concepts of conversion and missionary work as documented in Western European and North American historical experience. This experience may be different from, and so not directly applicable to, ancient Andean religious experience, for which there is essentially no archaeological evidence.

The growth in the importance of special sites as religious cult centres is not unique to Andean civilization. It is, however, a centrally important part

Above: The city of Pachacamac endured as a powerful centre of religious devotion to the supreme being for more than a millennium.

of ancient Andean belief from at least the Early Horizon. The central location of ceremonial complexes either within a domestic settlement or among surrounding domestic settlements began in the preceding Initial Period. Many sites are identified by scholars as pilgrimage sites: Chavín de Huántar, Cahuachi, Pukará, Tiwanaku, Pachacamac and Inca Cuzco itself.

THE PACHACAMAC MODEL
It is the Spanish colonial records describing the cult and oracle at Pachacamac that provide the basis for the model of ancient Andean pilgrimage and oracle sites. Essential elements of the Pachacamac model were a special chamber housing a cult idol, access to which was restricted to specialist priests; oracular predictions; public plazas for general ritual; and the establishment of a network of affiliated shrines in other communities.

CHAVÍN DE HUÁNTAR
The earliest widely recognized cult centre in ancient Andean civilization was Chavín de Huántar, for it appears to fulfil at least some of these criteria. Its complex architecture deliberately instilled a sense of mystery, supernatural presence and exclusiveness. First the Old Temple, then

the much larger New Temple, comprised numerous interconnected chambers holding a cult monolith carved with the symbolic image of a supernatural being. Its isolation within the temple clearly restricted access to it and made it more awesome and powerful. Its complex symbolic imagery made it necessary for specialists to interpret it.

The Old Temple contained the Lanzón, or Great Image, monolith and the New Temple held the Raimondi Stela. The curious position of the former, piercing through the roof of one chamber to a hidden upper chamber, implies an oracular room. The acoustics of the water channels of the temples also implies the mysterious use of echoing and mimicry of the elements.

Both the Old Temple and the New Temple were accompanied by open plazas. These were wide, flat spaces between the arms of the U-shaped platform mounds, and within each was a sunken ceremonial courtyard: round in the Old Temple, square in the New Temple.

The imagery of several Chavín deities became widespread: the Staff Deity and feline and serpent imagery in particular. Yet, felines and serpents were common

elements in earlier cultures throughout an even wider area. Several sites, however, show imagery, though locally produced, that is identical to that from Chavín.

At Huaricoto, north-west of Chavín, the Early Horizon ritual precinct contained a carved stone 'spatula' depicting the deity of the Lanzón. There is also decorated pottery of Chavín design. Other sites in adjacent highlands also have portable artefacts of Chavín style. It may be, however, that the Chavín Cult was adopted in addition to established local patron deities.

More revealing is Karwa on the southern coast, near the Paracas necropolis site. Textiles from the Karwa tomb are

Above: The Inca trail has become a modern 'pilgrimage' route. This is the sentry post of Runkuaqay on the way to Machu Picchu.

decorated not in the local Paracas style but in the bright colours and images of the Chavín Cult, including their composition, bilateral symmetry and double profiling. The Chavín Staff Deity, here in female form and sometimes called the Karwa Goddess, is unmistakable. Such faithful adherence to the Chavín orthodoxy seems to betray Chavín presence or a shrine in a network of Chavín shrines.

In the northern highlands, Chavín stone sculpture from Kuntur Wasi and Pacopampa clearly displays Chavín imagery. In the upper Lambayeque river drainage, two matching carved stone columns were found, reminiscent of the Black and White Portal columns at Chavín de Huántar. Further, in the Chicama Valley there were painted adobe columns (now destroyed), one of which was painted with a winged creature like those on the Black and White Portal.

The distribution of these sites across cultural spheres and production zones indicates the establishment of Chavín shrines and may imply the integration of the cult into local community structures.

Left: Chavín de Huántar became the earliest widely recognized pilgrimage and oracular site in the Early Horizon.

161

TEMPLES AND SUNKEN COURTS

The earliest ceremonial complexes in the northern coastal valleys and adjacent northern Peruvian sierra organized both positive and negative space in the forms of platforms and sunken courts. The forming of a U-shape, comprising a tiered platform at the base and two elongated platform wings enclosing a sunken court and a level, open plaza around it, was clearly symbolic. The form was repeated at numerous coastal valley and northern and central Peruvian highland sites. Its mere repetition underlies a core of common religious belief.

U-SHAPE ORIGINS

The U-shaped ceremonial structure was the culmination of the development of two elements: platforms and subterranean courts. The U-shaped temple established at Chavín de Huántar as the centre of a religious cult had representations as far afield as the southern coastal valleys. But the form began much earlier, in the Initial Period.

The building of platform mounds began at least as early as 3000BC. The earliest were those at Aspero in the Supe Valley: the Huaca de los Idolos and the Huaca de los Sacrificios, among a ceremonial complex of as many as 17 platforms. Within the next few centuries

Below: The mud-plaster walls of the Middle Temple at Garagay feature a fanged being with spider attributes and water symbolism.

smaller complexes of mounds had been built at Piedra Parada, also in the Supe Valley, El Paraíso in the Chillón Valley, Río Seco in the Chancay Valley, Bandurria in the Huaura Valley, Salinas de Chao and Los Morteros in the Chao Valley, and at Kotosh, a highland site in the Río Huallaga-Higueras Valley.

Ancient Andeans were thus building ceremonial architecture as early as the first royal pyramids in Egypt and temple platforms, called ziggurats, in ancient Mesopotamia; and Andean ceremonial platforms are the earliest in the New World, predating the first Olmec earthen pyramids in Mesoamerica by at least 1,000 years.

Two 'traditions' of raised platforms developed, both based on ritual on top of the platform and open ceremonial space at the base for an attendant congregation: the Supe-Aspero Tradition and the El Paraíso Tradition. Chambers and niches to house ritual objects were built on top as the traditions evolved.

The practice of building circular sunken courts (*plazas hundidas*) also began in northern Peru during the 2nd millennium BC. Most often they were built in association with a platform at its base and aligned with the platform's staircase. Early examples include Salinas de Chao, Piedra Parada and highland La Galgada.

Above: The great temple pyramid platform of Huaca Larga incorporated La Ray Mountain in the centre of the Moche city Tucume Viejo.

Only occasionally was a sunken court built as the sole ceremonial element, for example at Alto Salavery.

By about 2000BC the stone-built civic-ceremonial centre at El Paraíso was the largest Preceramic Period civic-ceremonial centre on the coast. With a group of small temples forming a base and two elongated parallel platforms, it was a configuration transitional to the classic U-shaped structures of the Initial Period.

Below: Huaca de la Luna, mimicking the hill behind it, another Moche mud-brick temple of the Early Intermediate Period.

SECHÍN ALTO

By 1200BC the U-shaped ceremonial complex at Sechín Alto was the largest civic-ceremonial complex in the New World. At its fullest development it included all the elements of the classic U-shaped ritual centre. Construction began in about 1400BC (although one radiocarbon date from the site is as early as 1721BC). Its principal platform ruin still stands some 44m (144ft) above the plain and covers an area 300 x 250m (985 x 820ft). The huge U-shape is formed by sets of parallel platform mounds extending from the base corners of the pyramid, and forming part of a ritual area 400 x 1,400m (1,310 x 4,600ft). Running north-east from the principal pyramid is a succession of plazas and sunken courts.

The principal wings enclose a plaza with an early, small sunken court. Beyond the ends of these mounds there is a larger circular sunken court, then another open area formed by two long, thin parallel platforms flanking a plaza approximately 375m (1,230ft) square. Forming the end of the complex, 1km (½ mile) north-east of the principal platform, an H-shaped platform faces the main pyramid and flanks the largest circular sunken court, 80m (262ft) in diameter. The principal pyramidal platform is faced with enormous granite blocks set in clay mortar. Some of the blocks are up to 1.4m (4.5ft) on each side and weigh up to 2 tonnes (tons).

Surrounding the Sechín Alto complex there was 10.5 sq km (2,560 acres) of buildings and smaller platforms.

Above: The high stone walls of the rectangular Semi-subterranean court at Tiwanaku were decorated with stone trophy heads.

Like other U-shaped complexes, the site must have been a religious centre that served its surrounding area. Judging by its size, it may have served a considerable region as well.

RITUAL MEANINGS

The practical aspects of the arrangements of the U-shaped complex seem obvious: a raised platform from which to address a crowd, an open area for the crowd to stand in and a sunken court for exclusive ritual. There is an element of implied control in the arrangement: the congregation was partly confined between the arms of the U-shape, and their attention could be monitored from the height of the platform or focused on the sunken court.

Perhaps the two elements symbolize the concepts of a sky deity and an earth deity. Ritual may have involved procession from one to the other. Assuming strong naturalism in early Andean religious thought, the gods were believed to inhabit or infuse the natural landscape. Thus platforms were representative mountains and sunken courtyards representative valleys or caves. Further, their shapes might have represented the sky father and the earth mother, the womb and the symbolic shapes of man and woman. In seeming recognition of the source of life-giving water as the mountain thunder and rainstorms, the open ends of U-shaped complexes were oriented towards the mountains, their U-shapes imitating the collecting valleys.

Below: The ultimate sacred circular court of the great Sacsahuaman Temple of Cuzco formed the puma's head of the Inca capital.

SACRED CEMETERIES

Honouring the gods in the southern coastal desert cultures was focused on cemetery rites and ancestor worship. The dry climate has been instrumental in preserving the buried bodies and artefacts in the tombs.

SHARED TRADITIONS

The Paracas and Nazca cultures developed in continuous succession through the Early Horizon and Early Intermediate Period in the southern valleys and deserts of Peru, focusing their settlement and economy around sea fishing and shellfish collecting, and later on maize and cotton agriculture. Early Paracas ceramics and textile decoration shows much influence from Chavín de Huántar. At Karwa, near the early Paracas necropolis, textiles from an elite tomb are decorated with one of the best representations of the Staff Deity. Here she is the Staff Goddess, thought to honour a local goddess while at the same time acting as a 'wife' or 'sister' shrine to the Chavín Cult in the north.

Below: Stone slab circles at the Sillustani necropolis of the Colla people possibly served as the sites of burial ceremonies before bodies were taken to their kinship chullpa *tower.*

The Paracas and Nazca developed their own distinct style and deities. Quintessential was the Oculate Being, a wide-eyed distinctively local deity depicted in brightly painted ceramic masks and portrayed, flying, on pottery and textiles.

THE CAVERNAS CEMETERY

Paracas settlements covered an area of some 54ha (133 acres) around a core area of about 4ha (10 acres) on the low slopes of the Cerro Colorado on the Paracas Peninsula. Among the sprawling habitation remains, special areas were used as cemeteries for hundreds of burials, possibly the foci of family cults for nearby and more distant settlements.

Great care was taken in the burial of the dead in the Cavernas cemetery area. The naked corpse was tied with a cord into a flexed seated position. The body was wrapped in several layers of richly coloured textiles, both cotton and wool, revealing trade contact with highland cultures for llama wool. Placed in a basket and accompanied by plain and richly decorated ceramics, and sheet-metal jewellery, the whole was finally wrapped in plain cotton cloth. Such 'bundles' were

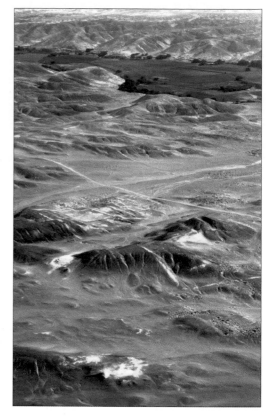

Above: Cahuachi, a sacred 'city' of about 40 temple mounds, served as a funerary and pilgrimage centre for Nazca religion.

then enshrined in large subterranean crypts, which were reopened and used repeatedly over generations, presumably by kin groups as family mausoleums.

PARACAS INFLUENCE

A prominent element in Paracas and Nazca religious ritual was decapitation. Trophy heads adorn pottery and stream from the waists of Oculate Beings on textiles. In addition, the skulls of many Paracas burials show evidence of ritual surgery, with small sections of the cranium being removed by incision and drilling. The exact purpose of this operation is unknown – it may have been ritual or medical. The Nazca inherited veneration of the Oculate Being from the Paracas culture.

Highland drought had caused increasing aridity in the coastal plains. It seems likely, therefore, that the Oculate Being was

associated with water and precipitation. Flying Oculate Beings perhaps betray a fixation with the sky. As a practical measure, the Nazca developed an elaborate system of underground aqueducts to collect and channel the maximum amount of water around Cahuachi. Great stepped spiral galleries, cobbled with smooth river stones, gave access to the wells.

Two of the most important Nazca settlements were Cahuachi and Ventilla, the first a ritual 'city', the second an urban 'capital'. Ventilla covered an area of at least 200ha (495 acres) with terraced housing, walled courts and small mounds. It was linked to Cahuachi by a Nazca line across the intervening desert.

Revealing their wide Andean contacts, Nazca ceramics and textiles are also decorated with a multitude of supernatural, clearly symbolic images. As well as sea creatures, crabs, insects and serpents that would have been familiar local sights, images of monkeys, felines and tropical birds from the rainforests were also used.

Below: In the Nazca cemetery (and Paracas, shown above) of the southern desert coast cultures, the desiccated conditions preserved the hair, fibres and textiles of the deceased.

The trophy-head cult extended to caches of trepanned, severed skulls of sacrificial victims being found among the remains in Nazca cemeteries.

LINES AND CEREMONIAL MOUNDS
Nazca religion is defined by two elements. Cahuachi was a ritual complex concerned with spiritual matters rather than daily life. Covering an area of 150ha (370 acres), it comprised a complex of 40 ceremonial mounds made by shaping natural hillocks into terracing and associated plazas. It was used from about AD100 to 550, and thereafter continued in use as a mortuary ground and place of votive offering. The entire site appears to have been devoted to mortuary practices, probably as family vaults following the Paracas tradition.

The largest mound was 30m (98ft) high, modified into six or seven terraces with adobe-brick retaining walls. Most of the tombs have been looted, but the few unlooted tombs excavated yielded mummified burials accompanied by exquisitely decorated, multicoloured woven burial coats and ceramics. Some contained animal sacrifices and ritual human sacrifices of Nazca men, women and children. Some skulls had excrement inserted into the mouths; some had been perforated and a

Above: The Paracas cemetery (and Nazca, shown below left) of the Early Horizon and Early Intermediate Period served numerous cities as kinship burial mausoleums.

carrying cord inserted; some had blocked eyes, cactus spines pinning the mouth shut, and tongues removed and put in pouches.

The second element was the Nazca lines, the geoglyphs forming geometric patterns, clusters of straight lines and recognizable animal and plant figures. There are some 1,300km (808 miles) of such lines, including 300 figures. A huge 490m-long (1,600ft) arrow, pointing towards the Pacific Ocean, is thought to be a symbol to invoke rains. The lines were undoubtedly associated with the Nazca preoccupation with water and crop fertility, together with worship of mountain deities – the ultimate source of water.

Cahuachi was abandoned as the coastal valleys became more arid. Simultaneously, there was an increase in the number and elaboration of Nazca lines. Regarded as ritual pathways, perhaps like the family vaults dedicated to kin groups, the increase in their use represents desperate efforts to placate the gods who had forsaken them. As Cahuachi was abandoned, people covered the mounds with layers of sand.

THE PACHACAMAC NETWORK

The religious network of Pachacamac was organized in sympathy with Andean concepts of community, mutual exchange, taxation and kinship.

THE ORACLE SITE

The cult centre was the city of Pachacamac at the mouth of the River Lurín, south of modern Lima. It comprised a complex of adobe platforms and plazas. An isolated chamber at the summit of the principal platform housed an oracle. There were open plazas in which pilgrims could fast and participate in public ceremony. Access to the oracle chamber was strictly limited to cult specialists. Oracular messages were given by these specialists concerning life and the future: predictions about the weather, favourable interventions of the gods with the elements, protection

Below: Pachacamac, established in the 3rd century AD, soon became a cult centre for the supreme deity, Pachacamac.

against diseases, specialized knowledge about the best times for planting and the harvest. Earthquakes, crop failure and other disasters were believed to be the result of antagonizing the god Pachacamac.

Much of what is known of the Pachacamac oracle site is from descriptions from Inca and early Spanish colonial sources. The elements of the central coastal ceremonial city incorporated the full range of Andean religious architecture: platform mounds, sacred compounds and plazas for congregational worship, and exclusive chambers for restrictive ritual performed by specialists.

Distant communities solicited the priests for permission to establish branch shrines to Pachacamac. If deemed to have the ability to support cult activities, a priest from Pachacamac was assigned to the new shrine and the community supplied labour on and produce from assigned lands to support him and the shrine. Part was kept for the shrine and

the rest sent to the Pachacamac oracle site. Such branches were thought of as the wives, children or brothers and sisters of the main cult complex.

THE CULT

Pachacamac – 'earth/time maker' – was the creator deity of the peoples of central coastal Peru and the adjacent Andes. The Pachacamac cult and shrine began to become important in the latter half of the Early Intermediate Period. By the 16th century a network of shrines spanned the range of Andean Area production zones from the coast into the highlands, as well as north and south along the coast.

The cult itself spread from the coast, first north and south, then inland into the highlands, where worship of Pachacamac rivalled the highland creator deity Viracocha. Its spread inland is associated with the inland spread of the Andean Area Quechua language.

In the Middle Horizon and Late Intermediate Period the cult and oracle site overtook the importance of local deities to the north and south coasts – those of the Nazca and Moche. Even when the mountain empire of Wari rose and its armies threatened the coast, ultimately to conquer Pachacamac and incorporate the city into its empire, Pachacamac remained independently important as an oracle site. In fact, despite being politically demoted to an outpost of Wari power, Pachacamac remained religiously important throughout the Late Intermediate Period.

When the Incas arrived in the Late Horizon they immediately recognized the importance of the oracle, not only locally but also throughout the region and beyond. They recognized Pachacamac's importance in relation to Viracocha and sought to accommodate the religious concepts that both gods embodied.

The cult thus endured for more than a millennium. In addition to its primary religious purpose, it became entrenched in

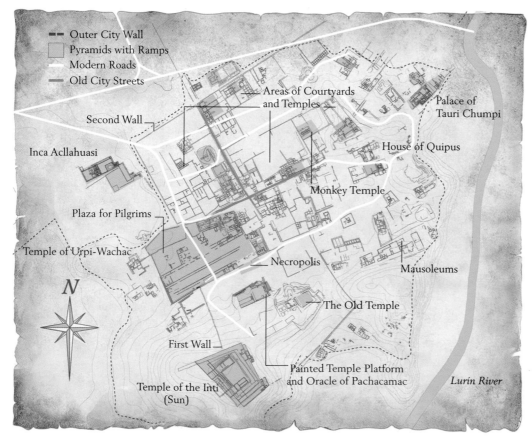

Outer City Wall
Pyramids with Ramps
Modern Roads
Old City Streets

Areas of Courtyards and Temples
Palace of Tauri Chumpi
Second Wall
House of Quipus
Inca Acllahuasi
Monkey Temple
Plaza for Pilgrims
Temple of Urpi-Wachac
Necropolis
Mausoleums
N
The Old Temple
First Wall
Painted Temple Platform and Oracle of Pachacamac
Lurin River
Temple of the Inti (Sun)

the community and its social structure, in its agricultural production and in the redistribution of wealth. There is, however, no recorded evidence of the use of missionaries to spread the cult's ideology.

EARLY ORIGINS

The site of Pachacamac became important locally from the latter half of the Early Intermediate Period, when the first phases of the pyramid platform to the sun and adjoining Temple to Pachacamac were built. It became an important political power during the Middle Horizon, and may have been partly responsible for the northern shift of Moche power in the late Early Intermediate Period/Middle Horizon.

Wari presence is attested by the architecture and a Wari cemetery, and the continuance of the site's religious importance is implied by a wooden post carved with figures of Wari-like divinities, as well as stone figurines. The upper part of the post depicts a man holding a bola and wearing a chest ornament; the lower part is carved with double-headed serpents, jaguars and a figure with attributes like those of the 'angels' on the Gateway to the Sun at Tiwanaku.

LATE HORIZON PACHACAMAC

The 16th-century chronicler Cieza de León noted the importance of the shrine and Inca reverence for it, while the 17th-century writer Father Bernabe Cobo devoted an entire chapter to a detailed description of the ancient site.

Cobo describes how devotees of the Pachacamac Cult visited the centre specifically to petition the priests there to establish satellite shrines in the cities of their homelands, and to permit them to erect 'wife', 'son' or 'daughter' shrines of their local deities, to Pachacamac. Prophecy from the oracle was sought for everything from health, fortune, the well-being of

Below: The Incas recognized Pachacamac's importance, but also built a temple to Inti, the sun god, here.

Above: The main pyramid platform at Pachacamac was surrounded by a vast complex of courtyards and platforms.

crops and flocks, the weather and even the prognosis of Inca battle plans. Defying or neglecting Pachacamac was believed to provoke earthquakes. Offerings in solicitation of oracles included cotton, maize, coca leaves, dried fish, llamas, guinea pigs, fine textiles, ceramic drinking vessels and gold and silver – no doubt useful to the priests.

The arrival of aliens – the Spaniards – caused the oracle to fall silent, although worshippers still visit Pachacamac today to make offerings.

THE SACRED CORICANCHA

The Coricancha or Golden Enclosure of imperial Cuzco, was the centre of the Inca cosmos. It was the supreme ceremonial precinct of the capital, the most sacred *huaca*. It housed the images of Viracocha, the creator, and Inti, god of the sun, and other principal Inca deities. From it emanated the sacred *ceque* lines, both physical roads and cosmic routes of sacred meaning. Forty-one *ceques* led to 328 sacred locations: *huacas* such as caves, springs, stone pillars and points on the surrounding horizon, and important locations such as critical junctions of the city's irrigation canals. One Spanish chronicler, Bernabe Cobo, listed 317 shrines.

These lines bound the Inca world, physical and religious, to the Coricancha 'navel' of the world. From points within the precinct, priests plotted the movements

Below: The sacred Coricancha included separate chambers dedicated to and housing the idols of the principal Inca deities.

of Mayu (the Milky Way) across the night sky – for example from the Ushnua Pillar, from which sightings of Mayu were taken between two pillars on the distant horizon.

The complex was in the tail of the puma image profile that formed the plan of Cuzco, at the confluence of the rivers Huantanay and Tullamayo, emphasizing the importance of water in the Andean psyche. The second most sacred shrine of the city, Sacsahuaman, formed the puma's head at the prominence above the rivers.

THE SACRED WASI

The complex is sometimes referred to as the Temple of the Sun (Inti), but in fact, the temple to Inti was one of several temples forming the precinct. It was built of stone blocks so carefully fitted together that there was no need for mortar. Its walls were covered with sheet gold – referred to as 'the sweat of the sun' – while another of the temples, to Quilla, was covered in silver ('tears of the moon').

Above: The entrance to the Golden Enclosure of the Coricancha in Cuzco, centre of the state cult of Inti (the sun god).

The precinct comprised six *wasi*, or covered chambers, arranged around a square courtyard. Each *wasi* was dedicated to one of the six principal Inca state deities: Viracocha, Inti, Quilla, Chaska-Qoylor (Venus as morning and evening star), Illapa (weather, thunder, lightning) and Cuichu (rainbow), ranged hierarchically in that order, although Viracocha and Inti were near equivalents.

Each temple housed an image of the deity and the paraphernalia of ritual and worship. A special room was reserved for the storage and care of the mummies of deceased emperors (*mallquis*). On ritual days – for example the winter and summer solstices of Inti Raymi and Capac Raymi – the *mallquis* were brought out in their rich vestments, carried on royal litters in procession around the capital and offered food and drink while court historians recited their deeds. The temple courtyard was also the venue for incantations to and the sanctification of *capacochas* – specially selected sacrificial victims. From the Coricancha they set out

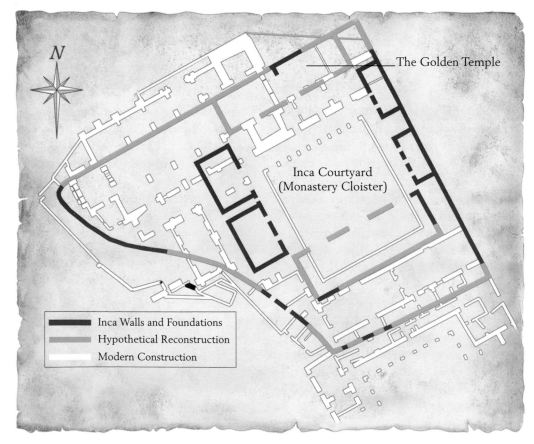

The Golden Temple

Inca Courtyard
(Monastery Cloister)

Inca Walls and Foundations
Hypothetical Reconstruction
Modern Construction

Above: Exterior of the Temple of the Moon in the Coricancha, Cuzco, showing the closely fitted blocks without mortar.

on their ritual journey following *ceque* lines back to their provinces, where they were sacrificed.

Other rooms were used to store the sacred objects taken from conquered provinces, including a *huaca* from each subjugated population. These *huacas* were kept in perpetual residence as hostages, and nobles from each subject population were forced to live in the capital for several months each year.

A GOLDEN GARDEN

The intimate mythological connection between Inti and gold was manifested in the temple garden. Here were gold and silver sculptures of a man, a woman, animals and plants representing creation. There were not only jaguars, llamas, guinea pigs and monkeys, but also birds, butterflies and other insects.

The arrangement of the Coricancha was established by the tenth emperor, Pachacuti Inca Yupanqui, in the 15th century, along with his rebuilding of much of the capital.

Something of its splendour was captured in the words of the conquistador Pedro de Cieza de León, as recorded in his *Crónica del Peru*, published in Seville between 1550 and 1553:

'[The temple was] more than 400 paces in circuit…[and the finely hewn masonry was] a dusky or black colour… [with] many openings and doorways… very well carved. Around the wall, half way up, there was a band of gold, two *palmos* wide and four *dedos* in thickness. The doorways and doors were covered with plates of the same metal. Within [there] were four houses, not very large, but with walls of the same kind and covered with plates of gold within and without…. In one of these houses…there was the figure of the Sun, very large and made of gold…enriched with many precious stones.

They also had a garden, the clods of which were made of pieces of gold; and it was artificially sown with golden maize, the stalks, as well as the leaves and cobs, being of that metal … . Besides all this, they had more than 20 golden sheep [llamas] with their lambs, and the shepherds with their slings and crooks to watch them, all made of the same metal. There was [also] a great quantity of jars of gold and silver, set with emeralds; vases, pots, and all sorts of utensils, all of fine gold.'

It was with this golden wealth of the Coricancha that Atahualpa attempted to secure his freedom when he was captured and imprisoned by Francisco Pizarro at Cajamarca in 1532.

Below: Each of the six deity chambers of the Coricancha temples was made with finely dressed stone masonry.

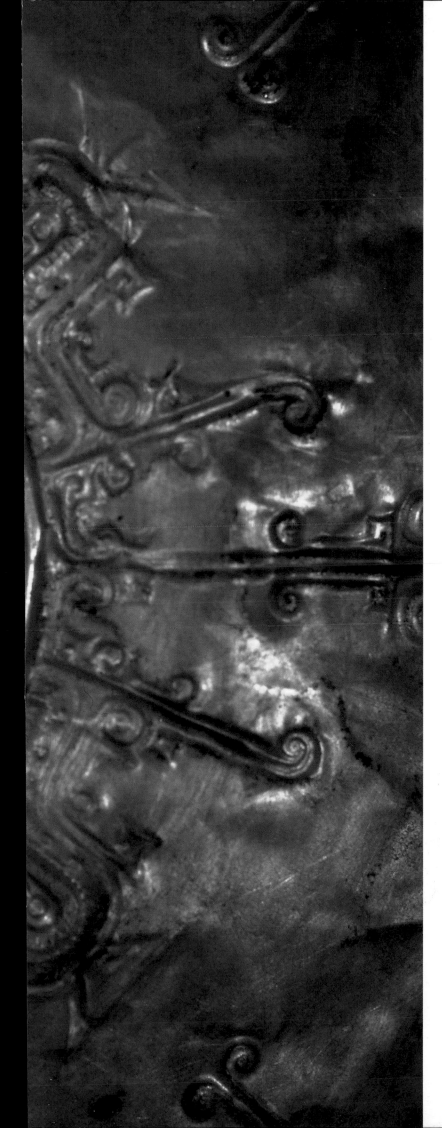

CHAPTER NINE

TALES OF THE GODS

Andean religious beliefs are replete with tales and stories of the deities and their representatives on Earth. However, it is not until the final stages of Andean history that we have this literature, and it is only because the stories were recorded by Spanish chroniclers, priests and administrators from their Inca informants.

These stories concentrate on Inca belief, creation and the rise of the Inca state. Some of the tales hark back to earlier cultures – those collected by the Inca in their conquests. For most of the pre-Inca cultures, however, we have only the archaeological evidence. For the Moche culture in particular, there is a rich 'narrative' of painted scenes on pottery, but most other imagery is of a more static than narrative nature. Nevertheless, an event in progress can be detected in the series of marching figures at Initial Period Cerro Sechín and in the tenoned stone heads on the walls of the temple court at Chavín de Huántar, showing the transformation of a shaman into a jaguar.

The use of creatures from distant, alien environments in the art reveals the contact of cultures across widely dispersed regions. By comparing the images with Inca history and mythological tales, it may be possible to find the origins of belief in pre-Inca cultures. Common imagery, modified through time, inevitably reflects continuity in belief.

Left: The face of the sun god on a gold dish made by a Manteño craftsman (Ecuador) at the far north of the Inca Empire.

SUN GOD AND MOON GODDESS

Ancient Andean traditions link the sun and moon as consorts, the sun being male and the moon female. Both were created and set into motion in the sky by Viracocha, the creator. His association with the sun in particular is made in the east–west orientation of his wanderings. The Islands of the Sun and of the Moon in Lake Titicaca were believed to be their birth places.

There is no doubt that the regular cycles of the sun and moon established recurrent, cyclical ritual calendars in ancient Andean cultures. The association of the sun with celestial matters and the moon with earthly cycles was probably reflected in the first ceremonial architecture – raised platforms symbolizing proximity to the sun and sunken courts providing links to the Earth.

Below: Silver and gold, 'tears of the moon' and 'sweat of the sun', represented an essential Andean duality.

The sun and moon were the epitomy of the Andean concept of duality. As opposites they represented light and dark, warmth and cold. However their importance to life and its everyday cycle was balanced, and thus they achieved oneness through the unity of their cycles.

Neither the Incas nor more ancient Andeans made obvious images of the sun or moon. Faces with radiating appendages are common but cannot be categorically identified as the sun. Images of a crescent moon, however, are found among the pre-Inca northern coastal Moche and Chimú cultures, hinting at a complex mythological tradition now obscure. It may be that the Inca suppressed the Chimú's closer association with the moon by their advocacy of the state cult of Inti, the sun.

AI APAEC AND SI

Among the Moche and Chimú the sky god Ai Apaec was perhaps combined with the sun. He was a somewhat remote and

Above: Niches in the interior of the walls of the Temple of the Moon at Pisac resemble those in the Coricancha in Cuzco.

mysterious creator god who, like Viracocha, paid little attention to the daily affairs of humans. Pictured in art as a fanged deity, his throne was regarded as being the mountaintops. His perception as a sky god appears to be implied by his association with a tableau of two scenes separated by a two-headed serpent. In the upper part appear gods, demonic beings and stars; in the lower part are musicians, lords, or slaves, and rain falling from the serpent's body, implying a celestial and terrestrial division.

Si was the Moche and Chimú moon goddess or god, sometimes regarded as the head of the Moche and Chimú pantheon. He/she was a supreme deity, omnipresent, who held sway over the gods and humankind, and controlled the seasons, natural elements, storms and therefore agricultural fertility. His/her origins can be traced to an un-named radiant and armoured war deity who rivalled or even replaced Ai Apaec in importance among the Chimú. One source refers to a Temple of Si-an dedicated to Si, interpreted as the Huaca Singan in the Jequetepeque Valley, possibly the structure known today as the Huaca del Dragón.

The Moche and Chimú realized that the tides and other motions of the sea, and the arrival of the annual rains, were

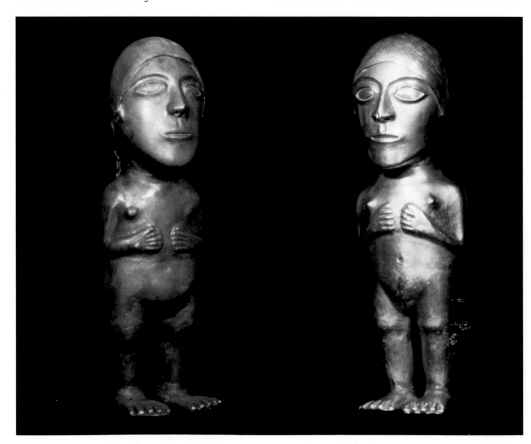

Above: The sacred Intihuatana Temple to Inti the sun god at Pisac, a palace city of Pachacuti Inca Yupanqui, north-east of Cuzco.

linked to the phases of the moon, and thus allocated great power to Si because the food supply and well-being of flocks depended upon his/her beneficence. In contrast, the sun was considered to be a relatively minor deity. Si was regarded as more powerful than the sun because he/she could be seen by both night and day, and eclipses were believed to be battles between the moon and sun. An eclipse of the moon was considered a disastrous augury and regarded with fear; an eclipse of the sun, however, was treated as a joyful occasion.

INTI AND QUILLA

The Incas specifically claimed descent from the sun, but refer less frequently to the moon as their mother, and her role in Inca creation myth is less obvious.

Nevertheless, the chronicler Garcilaso de la Vega describes the moon as sister and wife of the sun, and thus mother of the ancestral Incas.

The Incas worshipped Inti, the sun, but did not frequently portray him. The emperor was regarded as the 'son of the sun' and therefore Inti's embodiment on Earth. They associated the sun with gold, calling it the 'sweat of the sun', and the moon with silver, calling it the 'tears of the moon'. The sun and moon had separate chambers in the Coricancha Temple. The sun was represented by a sheet-gold mask with radiating gold appendages; the moon by a silver image in the shape of a woman.

The solstice days of Capac Raymi (summer/ December) and Inti Raymi (winter/ June) were auspicious days in the Inca ritual calendar.

The Inca empress was regarded as the earthly embodiment of the moon, Quilla, and in her role regulated lunar worship in the capital at Cuzco. A spring moon

festival was held in October. An eclipse of the moon was believed by the Incas to be an attempt by a huge celestial serpent or mountain lion to eat Quilla. During such events they would gather in force in their sacred precincts and make as much noise as possible to scare off the creature.

Below: The Temple of the Moon at Machu Picchu was formed from fine masonry and built within a natural rock overhang.

THE DECAPITATOR GOD

In a diamond frame, the grimacing face of a fearsome-looking half-human, half-jaguar peers from the walls of Platform I and the Great Plaza of the Huaca de la Luna at Moche. Stylized, stepped supernatural faces surround it, linked by a common 'thread' as if woven in textile. The face is outlined in red. Black hair and a beard curl from the head and chin. A sausage-shaped, down-turned mouth snarls, displaying human-like rows of white teeth and interlocked feline canines. His ears appear to be pierced and decorated with double ear-ornaments. Huge white eyes underlined in black and with heavy red brows stare menacingly with large black pupils. Curious, alien-looking miniature faces surround the head. This mural depicts the Decapitator God. What fear and reverence might he have struck in citizens as they stood beneath his gaze watching priests perform ritual sacrifice?

Below: Murals at the Huaca de la Luna depict a wide-eyed shamanic face with pierced ears, human teeth and feline canines.

RITUAL BLOOD-LETTING

The Decapitator God so graphically dominating the Moche capital was depicted in friezes and murals in temples and tombs, and on ceramics and metalwork at Moche and other north coastal valley sites, including Sipán in the Lambayeque Valley. He has several guises: as an overpowering face that grips one's attention, or full-figured, holding a crescent-shaped *tumi* ceremonial knife in one hand and a severed human head in the other. The elaborate plaster friezes at the Huaca de la Luna of Early Intermediate Period Moche are the most renowned, but the development of his imagery can be traced back to the Early Horizon in the preceding Cupisnique culture of the same region.

The Decapitator God is portrayed in an elaborate blood-letting rite painted on pottery and on temple and tomb walls. His role, acted out by priests, embodied

Above: There is no mistaking this sheet-metal and shell inlay depiction of the Decapitator God, with his grinning sinister expression, tumi *sacrificial knife and his latest victim's head.*

a gruesome sacrificial ritual. Although once thought to be merely representational of a mythical event, archaeological evidence discovered in the 1980s attests to its reality. An enclosure behind the Huaca de la Luna platform contained the buried remains of 40 men, aged 15 to 30. They appear to have been pushed off a stone outcrop after having been mutilated and killed. The structure, outcrop and enclosure seem to mirror the nearby Cerro Blanco and valley. Some skeletons were splayed out as if tied to stakes; some had their femurs torn from the pelvis joints; skulls, ribs, fingerbones, armbones and legbones have cut marks. Several severed heads had their jaws torn away.

A thick layer of sediment, deposited during heavy rains, covered the gruesome scene, and it is suggested that the sacrifice was performed in response to an El Niño event that might have disrupted the economic stability of the realm.

RITUAL COMBAT

The Decapitator God and sacrificial ritual are put into context by scenes painted on Moche ceramics and walls. Friezes show warriors in paired combat, almost always both wearing Moche armour and bearing Moche arms. The combatants are shown in narrative sequences: instead of killing a vanquished foe, the loser is next shown stripped and tied by the neck with a rope, being marched off for their arraignment. The final scenes show the captives naked, having their throats slit. Their blood is given in goblets to four presiding figures.

The most elaborate of these is the Warrior Priest. He wears a crescent-shaped metal plate to protect his back, and rattles hang from his belt. To his right sits the Bird Priest, wearing a conical helmet bearing the image of an owl and a long beak-like nose-ornament. Next to him is a priestess, identified by her long, plaited tresses, dress-like costume and plumed and tasselled headdress. The final figure, with a feline face, wears a headdress with serrated border and long streamers.

THE REAL THING

These scenes show ritual warfare in fields near Moche cities for the purpose of 'capturing' victims for sacrifices to the gods. Excavations in the 1980s of unlooted Sipán tombs in the Lambayeque Valley dated *c.*AD300 corroborate their actual occurrence. The elite citizens buried in the tombs, accompanied by sacrificial victims, were richly adorned and surrounded by the artefacts of sacrifice and ritual; the bodies were decorated with gold, silver, turquoise and other jewellery, and textiles. They wore

Right: A Chimú gold sacrificial knife handle, representing the legendary leader and conqueror Naymlap.

costumes identical to those of the four figures in the sacrificial ceremonies.

The principal body personifies the Warrior Priest. He wore a crescent-shaped back-flap and belt rattles, just as in the scene. The Decapitator God image decorates both back-flap and rattles – in this case the face is symbolized by a spider with a human face, perched on a golden web. The spider imagery is thought to reflect the parallel of the blood-letting and sucking the life juices of its prey. Offerings included three pairs of gold and turquoise ear-spools – one of which shows a Moche warrior in full armour – a gold, crescent-shaped headdress, a crescent-shaped nose-ornament, and one gold and one silver *tumi* knife. At the Warrior Priest's side lay a box-like gold sceptre, embossed with combat scenes, and a spatula-like

handle of silver studded with military trappings.

Near by, another tomb, less rich, contained the body of a noble with a gilded copper headdress decorated with an owl with outspread wings – clearly the Bird Priest. Sealed rectangular rooms near the tombs contained more offerings, including the bones of severed human hands and feet.

Two tombs dated *c.*AD 500–600 at San José de Moro in the Jequetepeque Valley contained the skeletons of women. Their silver-alloyed copper headdresses had tassels and other accoutrements of the priestess figure. Finally, at El Brujo in the Chicama Valley, a terrace frieze shows a life-size warrior leading a procession of ten nude prisoners by a rope placed around their necks. On a terrace above (later destroyed by looters) was a huge spider or crab with a fanged mouth and double ear-ornaments, one leg brandishing a *tumi* knife – the 'arachnoid decapitator'.

VIRACOCHA: THE SUPREME ANDEAN DEITY

Viracocha was the supreme deity, almost universally regarded throughout the Andean Area as the creator of the universe, the human race and all living things. He became a rather remote and inaccessible deity, although regarded as omnipresent and inescapable.

In Cuzco he was represented in his own shrine by a golden statue slightly smaller than life. He was white, bearded and wore a long tunic, as described by the Spaniards who first saw him there. In Inca legend, he travelled south to Cacha, c.100km (60 miles) south of Cuzco, where another temple and statue were dedicated to his worship. Another shrine and statue were at Urcos.

THE PRIMORDIAL CREATOR

To the Incas, Viracocha was primordial. He remained nameless, and instead was referred to by descriptive terms befitting his role in the various permutations of the creation myth. He was Illya ('light'), Tici ('the beginning of things'), Atun Viracocha ('great creator), or Viracocha Pachayachachic ('lord, instructor of the world'). The earliest Spanish chroniclers to describe him, Cieza de León and Juan de Betanzos around 1550, personify him, but to ancient Andeans 'he' represented a concept – the force of creative energy. The Quechua elements of his name, *vira* ('fat, grease, foam') and *cocha* ('lake, sea, reservoir'), can be rendered as 'sea fat', 'sea foam', or 'the lake of creation'.

As supreme deity, Viracocha's name has been used for the creator god in the pantheons of many pre-Inca cultures. Much of his history and legend therefore owes to the Inca's adoption of him from their conquered subjects. For example, his portrayal with weeping eyes was a characteristic almost certainly adopted from the weeping god imagery of Tiwanaku. In Inca legend he bestowed a special headdress and stone battle-axe on Manco Capac, the first Inca ruler, and prophesied that the Incas would become

great lords and would conquer many other nations. Viracocha Inca, the 15th-century eighth Inca ruler, took his name, presumably as representing strength and creative energy. As a concept, he could also be regarded as "shapeless" or "boneless".

CREATION AND LAKE TITICACA

Many Andean cultures believed that Lake Titicaca was where the sun, moon and stars were created, and that the lake waters were the tears of Viracocha acknowledging the sufferings of his creations.

Viracocha first created a world of darkness, then populated it with humans fashioned from stone. But he was disobeyed, so he destroyed them with a flood or by transforming them back into stones. These beings could be seen, it was

Above: Viracocha came to be associated with other sky symbols such as the double-headed rainbow serpent found in Chimú art.

thought, at ruined cities such as Tiwanaku and Pukará. Only one man and one woman survived, and were magically transported to Tiwanaku, where the gods dwelled.

Viracocha next created a new race of humans, and animals, of clay. He painted distinctive clothes on the humans and gave them customs, languages, songs, arts and crafts, and the gift of agriculture to distinguish the different peoples and nations. Breathing life into them, he instructed them to descend into the earth and disperse, then to re-emerge through caves, and from lakes and hills. These places became sacred, and shrines were established at them in honour of the gods.

The world was still dark, so Viracocha ordered the sun, moon and stars to rise into the sky from the islands in Lake Titicaca.

SPREADING CIVILIZATION

After his creations, Viracocha set out from the Titicaca Basin to spread civilization, but he did so as a beggar, bearded, dressed in rags, and under many names, and dependant on others for his sustenance. In other accounts he was described as a tall white man wearing a sun crown. Many of those he encountered reviled him. He was assisted by two of his creations, variously called his sons or brothers: Imaymana Viracocha and Tocapo Viracocha. The inclusion of the name 'Viracocha' imbued them with divinity and supernatural power.

He commanded Imaymana Viracocha to travel north-westward along a route bordering the forests and mountains and Tocapo Viracocha to journey northward along a coastal route. He himself followed a route between them, north-westward through the mountains. As they passed

Below: Temples were dedicated to Viracocha throughout the Inca Empire, as here at Rachi in the Vilcanota Valley.

through the land, they called out the people, named the trees and plants, established the times when each would flower and bear fruit, and instructed the people about which were edible and which medicinal. They taught humankind the arts and crafts, agriculture and the ways of civilization, and worked miracles among them, until they reached Manta on the Ecuadorian coast (the most north-

Above: A portrayal of Viracocha's face in sheet gold features typical Tiwanaku sun rays around the head, and weeping eyes.

western edge of the Inca Empire), where they continued across the sea, walking on the water until they disappeared.

Another version, recorded by Cristobal de Molina, begins with the world already peopled. A great flood destroyed all except one man and one woman, who were cast up on land at Tiwanaku. Con Tici Viracocha appeared to them and ordered them to remain there as *mitimaes* (people resettled by the Incas), then repopulated the land by making the Inca ancestors out of clay, and as before, giving them customs, languages and clothing.

This active role on Earth likens Viracocha to the preacher heroes in much pre-Inca legend. To the Incas, Viracocha remained remote, interacting with humans through other gods, particularly Inti, the sun god, and Illapa, god of weather. His purposeful travels relate to ancient Andean pilgrimage traditions. The trinity implied by the three Viracochas suggests a strong element of Christian interpretation in the descriptions of the Spanish chroniclers.

PACHACAMAC THE CREATOR

Pachacamac, 'earth/time maker', was the creator deity of the peoples of the central Peruvian coast. His Quechua root words, *pacha* ('time/space', 'universe/earth', 'state of being') and *camac* ('creator', 'animator') render him as potent as Viracocha and reveal lowland–highland association through the spread of Quechua from coastal regions to the Andes.

AN ANCIENT ORACLE

The centre of Pachacamac's worship was the pilgrimage city and oracle of the same name near modern Lima. The 16th-century chronicler Cieza de León noted Inca reverence for the shrine, and the 17th-century writer Father Bernabe Cobo describes it in detail. The Earth Maker was represented by a wooden staff (destroyed by Hernando Pizarro, brother of the conquistador) carved with a human face on both sides and housed in an oracular chamber, epitomizing the Andean concept of duality. Other carved wooden idols, which were scattered about the city, survive from other parts of the site.

Below: For more than a millennium, complexes of courtyards at Pachacamac accommodated pilgrims.

Pachacamac's following was ancient and widespread among central coastal civilizations, enduring from the Early Intermediate Period for more than a millennium. The oracle, like Early Horizon Chavín de Huántar, drew visitors from throughout the lowland plains and valleys, and the adjacent Andes. The principal temple platform was surrounded by a vast complex of courtyards and subsidiary platforms for the accommodation of pilgrims. Like Lake Titicaca and the Coricancha in Cuzco, it was one of the most sacred sites in the Inca Empire.

THE CREATION MYTH

There are many threads to Pachacamac's mythology. He was a serious rival to Viracocha. His cult developed independently and much earlier than that of Inca Inti, but the predominance of ancient contact between the coastal lowlands and the Andean highlands inevitably brought the two creator gods into 'contact' at an early date, long before the Inca compulsion to incorporate all their subjects' myths and pantheons of gods.

Mythology shows the two deities to have distinct identities, yet many similar traits: they created the world; they held control over the creation and destruction of the

Above: Guaman Poma de Ayala's depiction of a child sacrifice to Pachacamac in his Nueva Crónica y Buen Gobierno, c.*1613.*

first people; they travelled throughout the lands and taught, often in the guise of a beggar, and punished those who mocked them for this; they met, named, and gave their characters to the animals and plants.

In the principal myth, Pachacamac was the son of the sun and moon. An earlier deity, Con, had created the first people, but Pachacamac overcame him, and transformed the first people into monkeys and other animals.

Pachacamac then created man and woman, but, because he did not provide them with food, the man died. The woman solicited the sun's help, or in another version accused the sun of neglecting his duty, and in return was impregnated by the sun's rays. When she bore a son, she taught him to survive by eating wild plants. Pachacamac, jealous of his father (the sun) and angered by this independence and apparent defiance, killed the boy and cut him into pieces. He sowed the boy's teeth, which grew into maize; planted the ribs and bones, which became yucca, or manioc, tubers; and planted the flesh, which grew

into vegetables and fruits. The story appears to be a mythical précis of the discovery of cultivation among coastal peoples.

Not to be outdone, the sun took the boy's penis (or umbilical cord) and navel and created another son, whom he named Vichama or Villama. Pachacamac wanted to kill this child too, but could not catch him, for Vichama had set off on his travels. Pachacamac slew the woman instead and fed her body to the vultures and condors.

Next, Pachacamac created another man and woman, who began to repopulate the world. Pachacamac appointed some of these people *curacas* (leaders) to rule.

In the mean time, Vichama returned, found his mother's remains and reassembled her. Pachacamac feared Vichama's reprisal as the pursued became the pursuer, and he was driven, or fled, into the sea, where he sank in front of the temple of Pachacamac/Vichama. Wreaking further revenge, Vichama transformed Pachacamac's second people into stone, but later repented and changed the ordinary stone of the *curacas* into sacred *huacas*.

Below: The Incas established a temple to Inti (the sun god) alongside the ancient platform at Pachacamac.

SOCIAL ARRANGEMENTS

The second part of the tale explains the creation of social order among humans. Vichama asked his father, the sun, to create another race of people. The sun sent three eggs, one gold, one silver and one copper. The gold egg became *curacas* and nobles, the silver became women, and the copper egg became commoners. Thus, the world was populated. A variation describes how Pachacamac did the final deed by sending four stars to earth. Two of these were male, and generated kings and nobles; the other two were female, and generated commoners.

Other variations combine Con and Viracocha, emphasizing the latter's opposition to Pachacamac. The Huarochirí, between coast and sierra, incorporate Pachacamac's shrine, wife and daughters (including the seduction and attempted seduction of Pachacamac's daughters) into the itinerary of Coniriya Viracocha.

Such variations reflect lowland–highland and inter-coastal exchange and political tension. In the interests of empire, the Incas sought to alleviate any potential conflict by amalgamating the deities and by presenting variations as different names for the same events, as if it had always been so.

Above: Pachacamac was principally a coastal creator god who was ultimately combined with Viracocha, the highland creator deity.

INTI THE SUN GOD

The solstices were crucial days in the Inca ritual calendar. At Capac Raymi (summer/December), there was an imperial feast and initiation rites for noble boys; Inti Raymi (winter/June) honoured Inti, the sun, with feasting and the taking of important auguries. Plotting and confirming their dates was based on observations from the sacred Coricancha Temple in Cuzco.

THE CULT OF INTI

In Inca belief the sun was set in the sky by Viracocha, creator being of indistinct substance. The founding Inca ancestor, Manoc Capac, was believed to have been descended from the sun – the son of the sun – and this belief began the special relationship between the Incas and Inti. The adoption of the cult of Inti was associated especially with the ninth ruler, Pachacuti. Inca imperial expansion probably introduced a solar element into the mythologies of coastal peoples, as the father of Con and Pachacuti. Thus began the combining of creation myths with Inti, the sun.

Inti's image was most frequently a great sheet-gold mask, moulded as a human-like face, wide-eyed and showing a toothy grin. Sheet-gold rays, cut in zig-zags and ending in miniature human-like masks or figures, surrounded the face. Rayed faces were a common feature of pre-Inca

Below: The Christian Church of Santo Domingo, superimposed on the Coricancha Temple, dedicated in part to Inti.

Above: Llamas were frequently sacrificed to honour Inti, as depicted in this colonial painting of a sacrificial ceremony.

imagery, but their identification as the sun is not always tenable.

The sacred Coricancha precinct in Cuzco was the centre of the official state cult dedicated to Inti's worship. By the 16th century, the cult of Inti was so important that an incident witnessed by the priests during ceremonies in his honour appeared to foretell the fall of the empire. An eagle, mobbed by buzzards, was seen falling from the sky in the reign of Huayna Capac about 1526, coinciding with reports of the spread of an unknown, deadly disease from the north, now known to have been smallpox.

CAPTURING THE SUN

The emperor was seen as Inti's embodiment on Earth. Although regarded with awe because of his power, Inti was believed to be benevolent and generous. The sun was symbolically captured at special locations called *intihuatanas* ('hitching posts of the sun'), for example at Machu Picchu – carved stone outcrops probably used for astronomical observations. Together with set stone pillars,

priests used the shadows cast by them to observe and record regular movements of the sun in order to understand it and to predict the future. Solar eclipses were regarded as signs of Inti's anger.

INTERMEDIARIES

By the second half of the 15th century, as the empire reached the limits of expansion, Viracocha had become a remote deity, and Inti came to be regarded as his intermediary. Inca rulers emphasized this relationship carefully, and it became the basis for cultivating their intimate association with Inti. They became intermediaries between the sun and the people, and their presence was regarded as essential to assure light and warmth to make the world habitable. Elaboration and adoption of regional mythologies and combining them with Inca myth created an association between Inti, the emperor and power. Ceremonies and ritual offerings to Inti served constantly to reinforce this link.

Above: Perhaps the most celebrated intihuatana *is the one located at the highest point of the sacred city of Machu Picchu.*

THE RIGHT TO RULE

Historical and archaeological evidence shows that the expansion of the Inca empire beyond the Cuzco Valley began in earnest with Pachacuti Inca Yupanqui (1438–71) and with his son Tupac Yupanqui (1471–93). To unify the empire and convince their subjects of the Inca right to rule it became necessary to demonstrate a mythical common ancestry – namely the Inca ancestors. Thus, the first ruler, Manco Capac (at first called Ayar Manco), after emerging from the cave of Tambo Toco, acquired divine sanction when his brother Ayar Uchu flew up and spoke to the sun. Ayar Uchu returned with the message that Manco should thenceforth rule Cuzco as Manco Capac in the name of the sun.

Other versions of the creation myth name Inti as the father of Ayar Manco Capac and Mama Coya (also Mama Ocllo), and the other brother/sister/partners collectively known as the ancestors. Manco Capac and Mama Ocllo were sent to Earth to bring the gifts of maize and potato cultivation, establishing the Inca right to rule on the basis of their benevolence.

Below: The Intihuatana *or Hitching Post of the Sun at Machu Picchu was probably used for astronomical observations.*

A somewhat more sinister variation says that 'son of the sun' (Inti) was the nickname given to Manco Capac by his father to trick the populace of Cuzco into handing over power. Manco Capac wore gold plates to lend credulity to his divine dawn appearance to the people of Cuzco.

The emperor Pachacuti Inca Yupanqui's discovery of the crystal tablet in the spring of Susurpuquio, with its image of Viracocha, was followed by renewed construction and rearrangement of the sacred Coricancha, giving greater prominence to Inti. It was Pachacuti, too, who visited the Island of the Sun in Lake Titicaca, where ancient Andeans believed the sun to have been born. The construction of Sacsahuaman, at the north-west end of the capital, was probably also begun by Pachacuti. It became a sacred precinct and place of sacrifice to Inti, and probably also a site for cosmological observations. All these legendary events enhanced the importance of Inti and therefore the Incas.

195

CHAPTER TEN

CREATION AND THE FIRST PEOPLES

The creation story of the Ancient Andean peoples involved a layered world that revolved in endless cycles of creation and rebirth. They linked these concepts to their intimate association with their landscape to explain both its bounty and the difficulties and trials it sometimes presented.

The Spaniards recorded a wealth of rival, even seemingly contradictory, tales of creation among the peoples of the Inca Empire – and indeed throughout their New World colonies. However, as among the cultures of Mesoamerica, Andean cultural accounts of cosmic origin and the creation of humankind had common elements that arose from a long and common inheritance, strengthened by millennia of trading and social contact between highland and lowland peoples.

First was the belief that humanity originated at Lake Titicaca, and that Viracocha was the creator god. Second was the concept that, wherever they lived, a tribal group identified a particular place or feature in their landscape as the place from which they emerged. Third was a dual relationship between local people and a group of outsiders, which, whether it was portrayed as one of co-operation or conflict, defined the nature of how the groups interrelated. Finally, there was the conviction that there was a correct ordering of society and place in terms of rank and hierarchy.

Left: Lake Titicaca, with its sacred waters, came to be regarded by Andean peoples as the birthplace of the world.

CHAPTER ELEVEN

LEAVING THIS EARTH

The Incas regarded life and death as two of many stages in the cycle of being in which all living things took part. From birth through life and into death, there was a rhythm and sense of renewal. In a sense, in Andean belief one never 'left' the earth, for it was from the earth that people came (as described in the creation myth, when Viracocha created humans from clay, and also when they emerged from the earth into which he had dispersed them) and to it that they returned, becoming part of it at burial or remaining on it as a mummy preserved for ritual occasions.

Death did not always occur naturally, of course, and there is wide evidence of ritual sacrifice in an endless attempt to placate the gods. Once dead, rich and powerful ancient Andeans could expect an elite burial with all the trappings, possibly including mummification. Their bodies might be stored in family *chullpas* (burial towers) or buried.

The Lower World (the earth), or Hurin Pacha, was intimately linked to the World Above (Honan Pacha) and the World Below (Uku Pacha), the worlds of the gods, supernatural beings and spirits. Trained individuals, the shamans, could leave Hurin Pacha temporarily through the use of hallucinogenic drugs. They could travel in their altered mental state to converse with and seek help from the gods on behalf of individuals and the nation in general. In order to do so they could also transform into another being, for example a jaguar or an owl, taking on that being's perceived supernatural powers.

Left: Inca agricultural terracing on the steeply rising slopes above Bahia Kona on the Island of the Sun, in Lake Titicaca.

The richest elite burials ever found in the Americas were discovered in the Lambayeque Valley, where the Moche flourished in the Early Intermediate Period and early Middle Horizon, followed by the Lambayeque-Sicán culture of the later Middle Horizon and Early Intermediate Period. Neither used mummification.

ELITE BURIAL, MOCHE STYLE

The rich, unlooted tombs of the Moche Lords of Sipán were discovered by Walter Alva and Susana Meneses in the 1980s. The Sipán tombs reveal the riches and the exquisite craftsmanship of Moche metallurgy and ceramics. Yet Sipán was neither the capital nor the main focus of much Moche power during c.AD100–800. It is hard to imagine what riches have been lost that must have come from looted tombs, or that lie as yet undiscovered in unfound Moche tombs.

At Sipán, altogether twelve tombs were found in six levels of generations of burial. In the lowest level was the 'Old

Below: Ritual burials have been found beneath many Andean pyramid platforms, as here at Moche El Brujo.

Above: Early Intermediate Period Moche lords were elaborately buried in richly furnished tombs, only a few of which remain unlooted.

Lord of Sipán' and in the topmost level were the tombs of the 'Lord of Sipán' and of the Owl Priest. The levels of tombs contain burials, artefacts and depicted scenes that confirm the ritual scene images on the walls, ceramics, textiles and metalwork excavated at other Moche sites, especially the ritual sacrificial scenes painted on red-on-white ceramics and on murals. The Sipán tombs date from c.AD100–300. The offerings in the tombs and the costumes worn by the deceased are identical to those worn by the priests depicted in the sacrificial ceremonies.

LORDS OF SIPÁN AND OWL PRIEST

The principal body in Tomb 1, of the 'Lord of Sipán' – undoubtedly that of a local noble or regional ruler of the Lambayeque Valley – personified the Warrior Priest. He wore a crescent-shaped back-flap and

Right: Moche elite deceased were richly dressed and their faces covered with sheet-gold masks. This example has copper inlaid eyes and traces of red paint.

rattles suspended from his belt. Both back-flap and rattles are decorated with the image of the Decapitator God, in this case a human-like spider with a characteristic Decapitator fanged mouth and double ear-ornaments, perched on a golden web. The spider imagery is thought to reflect the parallel of the blood-letting of sacrificial victims and the spider's sucking of the life juices of its prey.

Offerings consisted of three pairs of gold and turquoise ear-spools (one of which shows a Moche warrior in full armour); a gold, crescent-shaped headdress; a crescent-shaped nose-ornament; and one gold and one silver *tumi* knife. At the Warrior Priest's side lay a box-like sceptre of gold, embossed with combat scenes, with a spatula-like handle of silver studded with military trappings.

Near Tomb 1, Tomb 2 contained offerings not quite so rich, but significantly including the body of a noble with a gilded copper headdress decorated with

an owl with outspread wings – clearly the Owl or Bird Priest of Moche friezes. Sealed rectangular rooms near the two tombs contained other rich offerings – ceramic vessels and miniature war gear, a headdress, copper goblets – and, even more tellingly, the skeletal remains of severed human hands and feet, probably those of sacrificed victims.

In the lowest levels, Tomb 3 contained the body of the 'Old Lord of Sipán', who lived about five generations earlier. His burial goods included two sceptres – one gold, one silver – and he wore six necklaces – three of gold and three of silver.

PRIESTESS FIGURES
Futher rich tombs confirming the accuracy of the Moche friezes and ceramic scenes come from San José de Moro in the Jequetepeque Valley. Here Christopher Donnan excavated the tombs of two women, which contained silver-alloyed copper headdresses with plume-like tassels, and other trappings of the priestess figure. These tombs have been dated to *c.*AD500–600.

Left: Repoussé-decorated sheet-gold kero *drinking cups from a rich Chimú burial. The one on the right shows warriors or possibly the ancient Chavín Staff Deity.*

ELITE BURIAL, SICÁN STYLE
The Sicán culture, which succeeded the Moche in the Lambayeque Valley, has produced equally rich tomb burials at Batán Grande, a few kilometres (miles) across the valley. Batán Grande was the largest Middle Horizon–Early Intermediate Period religious centre of the Sicán culture in the Lambayeque Valley. The ceremonial precinct comprised 17 adobe brick temple mounds, surrounded by shaft tombs and multi-roomed enclosures, with rich burials and rich furnishings reminiscent of the Moche Sipán lords' burial.

In the 1980s Izumi Shimada excavated the tomb of a Sicán lord at Huca Loro, one of the Batán Grande temple mounds, dated *c.*AD1000. The burial was of a man about 40–50 years old, accompanied by two young women and two children who had probably been sacrificed to accompany him. The lord was buried seated and his head was detached and turned 180 degrees, and tilted back to face upwards. He wore a gold mask and his body was painted with cinnabar. The grave contained vast numbers of objects – most of them gold, silver, or amalgamated precious metals (*tumbaga*) – arranged in caches and containers. The lord's mantle alone was sewn with nearly 2,000 gold foil squares. Other objects included a wooden staff with gold decoration, a gold ceremonial *tumi* knife, a gold headdress, gold shin covers, *tumbaga* gloves, gold ear-spools and a large pile of beads.

223

RITUAL SACRIFICE

Human and animal sacrifice was a common practice throughout ancient Andean civilization. It became a part of ritual from the Preceramic Period and continued into Inca times. Llama sacrifice was especially important in Tiwanaku, Wari and Inca ritual. The latter is an important scene in the Inca state creation myth. The founders sacrificed a llama to Pacha Mama before entering Cuzco. Mama Huaco sliced open the animal's chest, extracting and inflating the lungs with her breath, and carried them into the city alongside Manco Capac and the gold emblem of Inti.

SEVERED HEADS

These are perhaps the most powerful image of ancient Andean human sacrifice, and are a common theme in textile and pottery decoration, murals and architectural sculpture. Severed heads can be seen dangling from the waists of humans and supernatural beings in all ancient Andean cultures. As well as heads, other severed human body parts feature pictorially and in actuality in tombs.

The marching band of warriors on the monumental slabs at the ceremonial complex of Cerro Sechín is interspersed with dismembered bodies, severed heads – singly and in stacks – and naked captives. One warrior has trophy heads hanging from his waistband. One of the three adobe images at Moxeke is thought to represent a giant-sized severed head.

Severed heads form an important theme in the Chavín Cult, used both as trophy heads and as portrayals of shamanic transformation.

In Paracas and Nazca culture the Oculate Being has streaming trophy heads floating from its body at the ends of cords. Trophy heads feature frequently on Paracas and Nazca textiles and pottery. Real severed human heads were placed in Paracas and Nazca burials. There was

Above: A Nazca warrior or priest displaying a fresh trophy head – an integral part of ancient Andean religion.

a Nazca cult that collected caches of the severed and trepanned trophy skulls of sacrificial victims, and many human skulls have been modified to facilitate stringing them on to a cord.

DECAPITATORS

Titicaca Basin Pukará imagery also featured disembodied human heads. Some were trophy heads carried by realistically depicted humans; others accompanied supernatural beings with feline or serpentine attributes, thought, as in the Chavín Cult, to represent shamans undergoing transformation. The Pukará Decapitator sculpture is a seated male figure holding an axe and severed head, and the Pukará ceramic theme known as 'feline man' depicts pairs of fanged men lunging or running, facing one another or one chasing the other, each carrying a

Left: Nazca cemeteries included caches of skulls, many of which show trepanation and perforations for threading on to a cord.

Above: The Moche Pañamarca mural (restoration drawing) depicts the sacrifice ceremony, presided over by a priestess.

severed head and a staff. A cache of human lower jawbones found at Pukará indicates ritual sacrifice and/or warfare, either in the real or mythological world.

Images of the Decapitator God dominated temple and tomb friezes and murals in the Moche capital and are found at Sipán in the Lambayeque Valley, where the tomb of the Lord of Sipán was found. The nearby tomb of the Owl Priest contained boxes of offerings that included the bones of severed human hands and feet. Similar to the Pukará Decapitator, the Moche god holds a crescent-shaped *tumi* ceremonial knife in one hand and a severed human head in the other.

Tiwanaku and Wari craftsmen continued the severed-head theme in all media. The Akapana Temple at Tiwanaku incorporated a buried cache of sacrificed llama bones. Most of the human skeletons found buried on the first terrace and under its foundations were headless, and at the base of the western staircase a black basalt image of a seated, puma-headed

person (*chachapuma*) holding a severed head in his lap was found. Another Tiwanaku *chachapuma* sculpture is a standing figure holding a severed head.

The ultimate severed head is perhaps that of Atahualpa/Inkarrí, who was killed by the Spaniards. His body parts were buried in different parts of the kingdom, with his head in Lima. It is said that one day a new body will grow from his head, and the Inca emperor will return to revive the people's former glory.

SACRIFICIAL BURIALS

Human sacrifice became not only a part of religious ceremonies necessary to honour the gods, but also a ritual associated with elite burial, emphasizing the power and importance of the individual.

The earliest evidence indicative of human sacrifice comes from two burials at Late Preceramic Huaca de los Sacrificios at Aspero. The first was of an adult, tightly flexed with the joints cut to force the unnatural position and to fit the body into a small pit, wrapped only in plain cloth. The second was of a two-month-old infant placed on its right side. It wore a cloth cap and was wrapped in

cotton textile. Accompanying it were a gourd bowl and 500 clay, shell and plant beads. This bundle was placed in a basket, the whole wrapped in another layer of cloth, then rolled in a cane mat and tied with white cotton strips, and finally laid on two cotton wads. The assemblage was covered with an inverted, finely sculptured stone basin. The pair appears to commemorate the premature death of an infant of important lineage and a sacrificial victim to accompany its burial.

The Paracas Cavernas and Nazca Cahuachi cemeteries show numerous signs of ritual human sacrifice. Caches of skulls and trepanning have been mentioned. At Cahuachi it is obvious that some individuals were sacrificial victims. While honoured burials were mummified and accompanied by exquisitely decorated, multicoloured woven burial coats and pottery, sometimes with animal sacrifices, the sacrificial victims – men, women and children – had excrement inserted into the mouth, their skull perforated for threading on to a cord, their eyes blocked, and their mouth pinned by cactus spines or the tongue removed and placed in a pouch.

COMMEMORATIVE SACRIFICES

The roughly contemporary Moche culture of the northern coastal valleys practised a ritual of elite burial through generations as the huge Huaca del Sol pyramid was built in the capital, Cerro Blanco. A burial oriented north–south, as was the pyramid platform, was made near the base of the first phase of construction. Later burials were incorporated in successive phases as the platform was enlarged. There were several burials with mats and textiles within the adobe brick layers of the third phase, some of them of adolescents. Lastly, on top of the final construction stage of the fourth phase was an interment of a man and a woman, extended on their backs, accompanied by 31 globular vessels. The exact meanings of such burials cannot be known, but their association within construction phases of the huge platform was probably as sacrificial offerings for the well-being of the Moche people and their rulers.

Such a conclusion is strengthened by what can only have been a mass sacrifice behind the twin pyramids of Huaca de la Luna, also at Cerro Blanco. An enclosure at the base of the platform contained the mass grave of 40 men, aged 15 to 30, many of them deliberately mutilated. They may have been sacrificed to the gods during a time of

Above: As well as human sacrifice, animal offerings to the gods were a regular ancient Andean religious practice, performed at designated times of the year.

heavy rain caused by an El Niño event to solicit the return of good weather, for the sacrificial victims were covered in a thick layer of water-deposited sediments and the bones showed signs of cutting and of deliberate fracturing. As El Niño events occurred regularly in cycles, there may be other such mass sacrifices yet to be discovered.

The sacrificial scenes on Moche ceramics were actually performed by Moche lords such as the elite individuals known as the Lord of Sipán and the Owl Priest at Sipán. Judging by the frequency with which the scenes are shown on ceramics and murals, the ritual was a regular event, perhaps re-enacting a mythical story. The tradition of sacrifice appears to have survived the collapse of Moche power, even within the Lambayeque Valley, as illustrated in the sacrifice of two women and two children at later Lambayeque-Sicán Huaca Loro (Batán Grande).

CAPACOCHA SACRIFICE

The Incas associated red with conquest and blood. The chronicler Murúa says that each red woollen thread of the Inca

Left: Ritual sacrifice was performed by priests, perhaps impersonating gods or in shamanic 'transformation', as here, wearing a jaguar or puma mask.

state insignia, the Mascaypacha – a crimson tassel hung from a braid tied around the head – represented a conquered people and also the blood of an enemy's severed head.

The Inca practice of *capacocha* sacrifice was a ritual that continued these ancient traditions. As well as honouring the gods, it emphasized the power of the Inca rulers and maintained control over subjugated peoples. Specially selected individuals, usually children, from among the high-ranking *ayllu* kinship lineages of the provinces of the empire were brought to Cuzco to be prepared for the ritual. The selection was made annually and those chosen were destined to be sacrificial victims after ritual ceremonies in the capital. *Capacocha* sacrifices

Right: A Chimú ritual gold tumi *sacrificial knife, for slitting the throat of the victim, decorated with possibly feline heads.*

were offerings to either the sun god Inti or the creator god Viracocha, or to both of the gods. Momentous events such as war, pestilence, famine or other natural disasters could also provoke *capacocha* sacrifices.

In Cuzco, the chosen ones were sanctified by the priests in the Coricancha precinct, who offered the victims to Viracocha, and then marched back to their home provinces along sacred *ceque* routes that linked the provinces to the capital. The victims were sacrificed by being clubbed to death, strangled with a cord, having the throat slit before burial, or by being buried alive in a specially constructed shaft-tomb.

Capacocha sacrifices renewed or reconfirmed the bond between the Inca state and the provincial peoples of the empire, reasserted Inca overlordship and reaffirmed the hierarchy between the Inca centre and the provincial *ayllus*.

CAPACOCHA CHILDREN

Children were sometimes drugged with *chicha* (maize beer) before being sacrificed. Votive offerings usually accompanied the victim in death, such as elaborate clothing, male or female figures of gold, silver, bronze or shell dressed in miniature garments, llama figurines and miniature sets of ceramic containers.

The victims were sometimes carried up and left on high mountaintops regarded as sacred *huacas*, where their bodies

Left: A deer sacrifice performed by Death as a skeleton, displayed on a Moche ceramic stirrup-spouted ceremonial vessel.

would sometimes become preserved in the cold dry conditions that prevailed at such high altitudes. Famous examples include those at Cerro el Plomo in the Chilean Andes, Mount Aconcagua on the Argentinian–Chilean border, Puná Island off the coast of Ecuador, the 'ice maiden' at Mount Ampato and the two girls and a boy sacrificed and buried on Mount Llullaillaco.

227

MUMMIES AND MUMMIFICATION

This preservative treatment of the human body before burial, or even as a state precluding burial, was the ultimate ancient Andean expression of ancestor reverence. It was not an attempt to cheat death on Earth, nor a denial of the cycle of life, but rather an act of recognition of the next stage in the cycle. It was a preparation for the journey and a method of preservation that maintained the contact between those living in this world and those who had moved on to the next stage. In fact, mummification was not necessarily always achieved deliberately, but could also be the result of climatic conditions, since the desiccating conditions of the desert would preserve exposed bodies. In the same way, desiccation and freeze-drying methods used to preserve stored foodstuffs had been discovered by the ancient Andeans probably accidentally originally, and then deliberately applied.

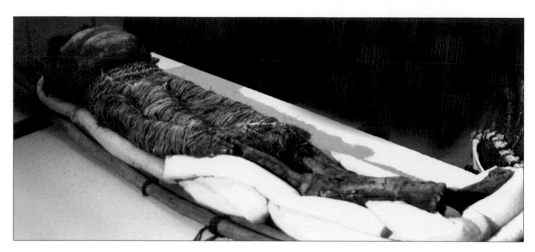

Above: Cinchorros mummifiction in northern coastal Chile predates Egyptian burials by some 500 years.

THE CHINCHORROS MUMMIES

The earliest mummification in the world was practised by the people of the Chinchorros culture in the Chilean Atacama Desert, starting about 5000BC. The Atacama is one of the bleakest places on Earth and officially recognized as the driest.

Mummification by the Chinchorros predates the earliest Egyptian mummification by about 500 years. It also demonstrates the beginnings of differentiation in burial practices within their community by the special treatment of chosen individuals. Most Chinchorros dead were buried in earthen graves without special treatment. About 250 individuals, however, had been preserved. Curiously these earliest mummies were not of revered elderly members of society; rather the majority of them are of newborns, children or adolescents.

Chinchorros 'morticians' perfected a high degree of skill. The deceased body was left exposed to decompose then completely de-fleshed. Cerebral and visceral matter were extracted and the

Left: Removal of the soft material, salting and careful wrapping helped to preserve organic materials in Paracas burials.

Above: A richly coloured Paracas woollen burial wrap, decorated with felines and perhaps the face of the Oculate Being, reveals the high status of a burial.

skin treated with salt to help preserve it. The bones were then reassembled as in life and secured in their positions with cords and cane supports. The form of the body was then replaced with fibre, feather and clay stuffing, held inside the skin, which was stitched in sections at the tops of the arms, wrists, torso, abdomen, groin, knees and shins as necessary. A clay death mask was applied to the skull, complete with sculpted and painted facial features, and a coating of clay applied to the body to delineate fingers and toes, with painted finger- and toenails. A wig of human hair was often attached as well. The result was a stiffened, statue-like form.

There is variation in treatment, presumably owing to individual skill and developments in preservation methods over generations.

The mummy was kept above ground as a continuing family member. Some mummies show surface damage, which in some cases was repaired. The preserved cadavers were clearly kept accessible for some time before finally being buried. Some burials were in family groups of adults and children. One such interment spanned three generations from infants and children to mature adults and a few very aged adults.

The inclusion of infants and children, especially separately or in group burials of the young, seems to rule out specific ancestor worship. However, the development of social hierarchy and perhaps lineage privilege is shown by the selection. Presumably special treatment and inclusion above ground within the community continued until the lineage no longer merited a distinct social position, at which time the mummy was then buried in an earthen grave.

LA PALOMA

The Chinchorros mummies were not the only ancient Andean attempts to preserve the body after death. The Preceramic site of La Paloma on the central Peruvian coast in the Mala Valley was short-lived, but comprised three superimposed settlements with some 4,000 to 5,000 circular huts in total. Abandoned huts later served as graves in which, from as early as about 4000BC, corpses were treated with salt to deter putrefaction. In combination with the dry coastal desert climate, the bodies were desiccated and stiffened as whole forms. At the time, such treatment contrasted sharply with the burial of disarticulated bodies in tropical and other areas.

THE ESSENCE OF PRESERVATION

Even these earliest methods of mummification seem to recognize the concept of essence. The methods do not attempt to halt decomposition of the flesh. Rather they preserve the essence of the earthly form, presumably in order to provide a 'vessel' for the journey of the spirit, or 'vital force', that ancient Andeans believed to be the next stage in the cycle of life. In Inca times, mummies were the preferred symbol of corporate identity and kinship solidarity. The Chinchorros and La Paloma peoples' early efforts at mummification reveal the antiquity of Andean belief that an intact body vessel was critical for the spirit to be able to enter the afterlife and join the world of the ancestors.

The elite burials of the north-coast Moche Sipán lords and later Sicán lords in the Lambayeque Valley were not deliberately mummified. The tradition of elaborate trappings certainly prevailed, but there was no deliberate mummification of the bodies. Their exquisite garments and tomb furniture did not, in the long term, preserve the bodies of the deceased lords, but their dress and grave goods certainly reveal a desire to prepare them and supply them for their journeys into the afterlife.

THE PARACAS/NAZCA MUMMIES

The traditions and concepts established at Chinchorros and La Paloma continued at Early Horizon Paracas and Early Intermediate Period Nazca, about halfway along the coast between the two Preceramic sites. The elaborate mummy bundles interred in the three Paracas

Below: Richly dyed multiple layers of cotton and woollen burial textiles and a feathered headdress emphasize the importance of this Paracas individual.

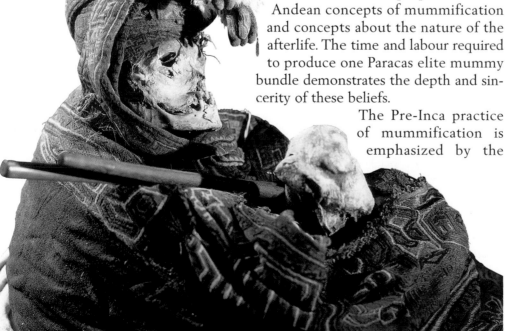

cemeteries – Cavernas, Cabeza Larga and Necropolis – and the Nazca Cahuachi cemetery show a multi-layered established social hierarchy, clearly defined by the levels of treatment in burial. The dry desert climate was a significant element in preservation, while the elaborate treatment of Paracas and Nazca corpses in multiple layers of burial textiles protected the mummies from deterioration. Social position was indicated by the size and elaboration of the mummy bundle. Once again, the treatment was to provide a vessel for the journey into the afterlife.

The attention to detail in procedures and the multiple layers of textiles and other trappings in Paracas and Nazca burials have been described above. The importation of foreign objects and materials in Paracas and Nazca graves – including exotic shells and llama wool garments, as well as the native-grown cotton textiles – reveals the extent of contact and trade between the coast and other regions, both sierra and tropical. It is significant that with such long-distance communication must have come ideas as well as objects and commodities, and it is this factor that perpetuated the Andean concepts of mummification and concepts about the nature of the afterlife. The time and labour required to produce one Paracas elite mummy bundle demonstrates the depth and sincerity of these beliefs.

The Pre-Inca practice of mummification is emphasized by the

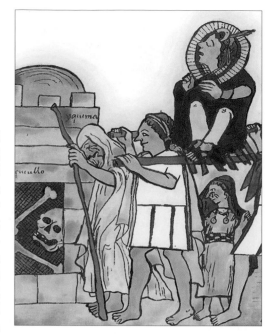

discovery of a row of mummy bundles *Above: An Inca mummy bundle borne on a litter for deposit in a mausoleum, from which it could be brought out on ritual occasions.*

in the burial of the puma-headed priest (*chachapuma*) beneath the summit structures of the Akapana platform at Tiwanaku. The priestly mummy's importance was accentuated by a row of mummies facing him in the tomb.

CHIMÚ/INCA MUMMIFICATION

Late Intermediate Period Chimú and Late Horizon Inca mummification was the culmination of the long tradition of Andean preservation of the body for the afterlife. Chimú and Inca mummification was achieved in a manner essentially the same as the methods developed by the Paracas people, the critical elements being desiccation and an elaborate mummy bundle of textiles and elaborate garments and jewellery, including precious metals and exotic items. Embalming included the use of alcohol – *chicha* beer made from the maize cultivated in a field near Cuzco was produced expressly to embalm the body of the ancestor Mama Huaco and was used for the succeeding Inca Qoya empresses.

INCA *MALLQUIS* MUMMIES

Every Inca community would have had its special *mallqui* (as it was called in the central and northern Andes) or *munao* (as it was called along the central coast).

The *mallqui* mummy was the community-level founding ancestor, the protohuman descendant of the deities – the great *huacas* such as Inti (the sun) or Illapa (thunder and lightning). In time, the term was applied to more recent ancestors of the kin group. Alongside *mallquis*, ancestors could also be 'mummified' in a transformed state: ancestors who had been petrified and who stood in sacred locations around the landscape. These were known as *huancas*, *chacrayocs* and *marcayocs*. Like the *mallquis*, these stone ancestors represented the first occupation of the region and the first *ayllu* kinship group called out by Con Tici, Imaymana or Tocapo Viracocha at the time of creation.

Inca *mallquis* were commonly kept in caves or in special rooms near the community. Some caves were reported by Spanish priests to hold hundreds of mummified ancestors. The Inca royal mummies – both the Sapa Inca (Inti) and the empress Qoya (Quilla) – were housed in special rooms in the Coricancha Temple in Cuzco, to be brought out on auspicious occasions and festivals and included as 'living' members of the royal household. After the Spanish Conquest they survived, hidden by Incas reluctant to relinquish ancient beliefs, until the late 16th century, when Spanish priests and administrators finally tracked them down and burned them as heretical.

CHIMÚ ROYAL MUMMIES

The immense Chimú capital at Chan Chan in the Moche Valley had at its core the walled city of *ciudadellas*, which housed the living and dead royal households of the Chimú kings. Each *ciudadella* compound comprised a 'city within the city' to accommodate the mummified remains of the king and both dead and living retainers. They 'lived' in rooms on special platforms, including labyrinthine divisions and thousands of storerooms and niches, and even miniature U-shaped ceremonial structures harking back to the most ancient cultures of the north coast.

FREEZE-DRIED MUMMIES

Another type of mummification occurred, perhaps intentionally, in the desiccated climatic condition of remote mountaintops. These were the *capacocha* child and young adult victims of the Inca ritual sacrifice of chosen representatives from the provinces of the empire. Cold storage of sierra agricultural production was a long-standing practice, complementing the

Above: A Middle Horizon Wari mummy bundle. They were preserved and brought out on special occasions by most Andean cultures from the Early Horizon onward.

hot, dry conditions used to dry foods by desert cultures. In the remote, dry, cold high-sierra locations of *capacocha* sacrifice and burial, the combination of elaborate bundling in textiles and the climatic conditions naturally preserved the bodies. The locations and the intent to revisit the *huacas* thus created by the sacrifice indicates that preservation through mummification was counted upon.

ANCESTOR WORSHIP

Reverence for one's *ayllu* kinship ancestors was integral in Inca society regardless of social rank. Special veneration was given to nobles and supreme respect to the royal pair. The enshrined mummies of the Incas and their Qoya wives were carefully tended. Even today the skull of an ancestor is kept in some Andean households to 'watch over' it and its occupants.

Signs of pre-Inca ancestor reverence are evident in the elaborate preparation and care of bodies in Paracas and Nazca cemeteries; especially revealing is the continued reopening of tombs to inter new family members or the maintenance of access to *chullpa* towers for the same purpose. Like so many practices in Andean civilization, the intensity of ancestor worship reached its most vivid and demonstrative phase among the Incas, who, with the Chimú, developed substantial industries around ancestor worship.

THE ROLE OF *MALLQUIS*

The mummified remains (*mallquis*) of Chimú and Inca rulers and their queens were cared for by dedicated cults. At Chan Chan they were housed in the *ciudadella* compounds. The cults of Inti and Quilla were housed in the Coricancha precinct in Cuzco. The *acllas* (chosen women) of Inti not only tended the *mallquis* of former Sapa Incas but were also the concubines of the reigning Sapa, thus forming a worldly link between the ancestors and the living Inti.

Every *ayllu* maintained mummified ancestor bundles and housed them carefully in special buildings or in nearby caves. *Mallquis* were believed to be the repositories of supernatural powers. As founding ancestors they were regarded as revered divinities, or representatives of the gods, and infused with *camaquen* – the vital force of all living things. They were able to transfer *camaquen* to crops to make them grow and to llama herds to make them multiply. Legendary exploits of *mallquis* were told about their ability to sustain agricultural production. They were responsible for the introduction of the different regional crops and for maintaining the fertility of the land. They had taught the people the different methods of agriculture such as irrigation and terracing to increase production.

Such beliefs maintained established land rights and the mutual obligations within and between *ayllu* kinship groups. They helped to co-ordinate labour between groups, communities and regions.

CONSULTING THE FOREBEARS

Inca ancestor mummies were consulted for numerous reasons, both for everyday concerns and on ceremonial occasions on issues of vital importance. They were consulted before undertaking a journey outside the community, for naming and marriage ceremonies in the life cycle, and on auspicious dates in the agricultural calendar such as sowing and harvesting.

On these occasions they were brought out to participate in the ceremony. They were dressed in fresh clothing, offered food and drink, and generally treated as living, active members of the community. Songs and dances were performed before them and the stories of their exploits told.

Left: An Inca carved wooden head with shell inlay eyes, dressed in dyed textiles – probably from a mummy bundle or more probably a huauque *double.*

Right: Ancestor worship began as early as the Nazca, who placed generations of the deceased in mausoleams and had kinship areas at ritual sites such as Cahuachi.

Spanish attempts to eradicate what they regarded as idolatrous beliefs were fiercely and secretively resisted. Local-level ancestors were considered crucial to community coherence, and most survived well into the 17th century.

HUAUQUES

The Quechua word *huauque* means 'brother'. The term was especially applied to man-made doubles – statues made in the images of the ruling Sapa Incas and other chiefs and nobles during their lifetimes. In his *Historia del Nuevo Mundo*, Bernabé Cobo describes these effigies as well dressed and of various sizes, and says that they were held equivalent to the imperial and noble *mallquis*. They included hollows wherein parts of the reigning emperor were placed when he

Below: As the Incas were so attached to their mummies and ancestor worship, here depicted by an ancestor mummy on a litter, it took the Spaniards over a century to stamp it out.

was alive, such as trimmings from his hair or fingernails. Upon his death the ashes of his burned viscera were usually put into the hollow. Many such duplicates were hunted down by the Spaniards and destroyed along with the actual mummies.

*Huauque*s were made of different materials and had more refined characteristics according to rank. The *huauque* of the upper division of an *ayllu* would have proper facial and other human-like features. That of the lower division would have amorphous or animal features. The *huauques* of earlier Sapa Incas were made of stone while those of the later rulers were made of gold.

After the Sapa Inca's death his royal *panaca* corporation undertook the care of his *mallqui* and *huauque*. During another emperor's lifetime such statues could be used as *mallqui* substitutes, especially on occasions when the real

mummy might be at risk of damage, such as on a long journey or when the living emperor was on a campaign of conquest. The loss of such an idol would be less serious than the actual destruction of a *mallqui*, for loss of the latter would amount to a state disaster: it would mean the loss of the *panaca's* identity.

A *huauque* could also represent a mythical ancestor. In this case invented descent could be confirmed by the effigy for political expediency. Once again, Inca practice appears to follow ancient Andean traditions. The greenstone idol Yampallec of the Sicán ruler Naymlap accompanied him in his conquest of the Lambayeque Valley, and the attempt of his descendant Fempellec to remove the idol was fiercely and successfully resisted by the priests who constituted the royal *panaca*. Nevertheless, the dynasty ended with Fempellec when the priests disposed of him.

TRANCES AND TRANSFORMATION

The ancient Andean cycle of life included trances and transformations during which life on earth was left and other worlds or states of being were entered.

TRANSFORMATIONAL STATES

Some temporary states of being could be experienced by everyone: for example near-death conditions, deep sleep, fainting and drunkenness. More profound states, such as transformation in order to commune with the spirit world, however, were usually drug-induced and were the realm of the shamans and high priests.

Below: This Moche effigy vessel depicts a jaguar-attired shaman with a jaguar emerging from his head.

That such beliefs, like most Andean religious concepts, were ancient is shown in the series of transformation sculptures at Chavín de Huántar in the circular sunken court of the New Temple. These portray a classic trip – the transformation of a human shaman into a revered jaguar. During such a transformation the shaman acquired the powers and wisdom of the animal into which he or she was changed.

Other states of transformation included the conversion of animals and of human heroes or deities into stone, to become sacred regional *huacas*. The reverse could also happen: stones or other features of the landscape could temporarily transform into living beings. The classic example is the calling upon the gods by Pachacuti Inca Yupanqui for help against the Chanca assault on Cuzco, traditionally in 1438. The gods transformed the stones of Pururaucas field into warriors. After the defeat of the Chancas, Pachacuti ordered that the stones should be gathered and distributed among the capital's shrines.

The Moche mural known as the 'Revolt of the Objects' represents another transformational theme – that of everyday objects sprouting limbs and humans with animal heads. This mythical story of the world gone mad and then returned to order was still told in Inca times and recorded by the Spaniards.

SHAMANSIM

This is the term used to describe a person who has special powers, usually aided by hallucinatory plant drugs, to gain access to the spirit world. In ancient Andean cultures the role of the shaman was crucial in everyday life. Priests of the most important temples, including the retainers of the most important oracles and shrines, such as Chavín de Huántar, Pachacamac and the

Above: On a stirrup-spouted vessel, a shaman wearing a jaguar headband and mushroom cap treats a woman with his healing touch.

Island of the Sun, were supreme shamans, but every local community would have had their local shaman as well. While the high priests served as intermediaries between the community and the lofty world of the gods, local shamans were consulted for everyday issues such as sickness and fortune.

Shamans in transformational states or in drug-induced states of being have been depicted in Andean cultures from the time of the building of the earliest dedicated ceremonial precincts. Such duality

*Above: The San Pedro cactus (*Trichocereus pachanoi*) was, and is, a rich source of vision-producing mescaline.*

in being is perhaps expressed in the symbolic crossed-hands friezes of the temple walls at Preceramic Period Kotosh. At the Initial Period coastal sites of Garagay, human–animal transformation is depicted in images of insects with human heads, and at Moxeke the earliest representation of shamanic trance may be represented by the adobe sculptures. Spiders with human heads, frequently depicted in the Moche and other cultures, were symbolic as predictors of the future, especially on climatic matters. Moche effigy pots even depict scenes of shamans at work, bent over their patients lying prone before them.

Below: A northern Moche ceramic figurine from the Vicus region shows a shaman clearly in a trance, sporting enhanced feline canines.

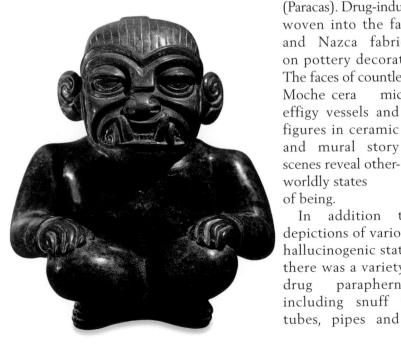

The role-taking of humans as deities in scenes of ritual is most famously depicted in the sacrificial scenes on Moche pottery and murals showing the Warrior Priest, Owl Priest and a priestess re-enacting the blood-letting ritual after symbolic combat.

HALLUCINOGENS

Shamanic transformation and trance for curative or special powers was normally induced through the use of hallucinatory plant drugs. The most common hallucinogens were coca leaves (*Erythroxylon coca*), coca incense, the San Pedro cactus (*Trichocereus pachanoi*) (the source of vision-producing mescaline), tobacco and various tropical mushrooms.

Classic characteristics of a hallucinogenic trance are shown in the adobe sculptures of Moxeke and Huaca de los Reyes: jawless lower mouth and/or fangs, flared nostrils and wide eyes with pendent irises. Such symbolic imagery is prolific in Chavín art and widely distributed in the northern and central Andean and coastal regions, and farther south at Karwa (Paracas). Drug-induced stares were woven into the faces of Paracas and Nazca fabrics and on pottery decoration. The faces of countless Moche ceramic effigy vessels and figures in ceramic and mural story scenes reveal otherworldly states of being.

In addition to depictions of various hallucinogenic states, there was a variety of drug paraphernalia, including snuff trays, tubes, pipes and small

knives for chopping. Coca leaves were chewed in a complex, many-staged ritual connected to war and sacrifice. Coca was also frequently used, along with *chicha* beer, to drug sacrificial victims before dispatching them.

Drug paraphernalia has frequently been found among grave goods, but a unique cave burial of a local medicine man, herbalist or shaman of the Callahuaya people, dated to the latter half of the 5th century AD, was found near Huari. He was accompanied by the tools of his practice: a wooden snuff tablet decorated with a Tiwanaku 'attendant angel' figure with a trophy head on its chest; a basket with multi-coloured front-facing deity figures; and various herbal plants that would have been used in his trade.

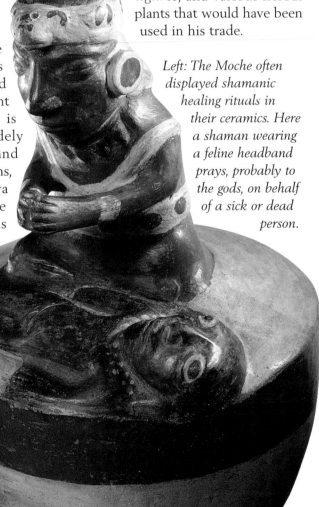

Left: The Moche often displayed shamanic healing rituals in their ceramics. Here a shaman wearing a feline headband prays, probably to the gods, on behalf of a sick or dead person.

CHAPTER TWELVE

A NEW GOD

Conversion of the peoples of Mesoamerica and South America began shortly after Columbus landed on the islands of the Caribbean Sea. Once it was realized that he had not sailed west and reached the Orient, the Christian kings and queens of Spain and Portugal and their clergy saw a ripe new world for conversion to the path of Christ.

Many concepts in Christianity – in this case Spanish Catholicism – were ideas not unfamiliar, superficially, to ancient Andean beliefs. Similarly, Christian priests interpreted various elements in the mythical stories related to them by their converts as aspects of or vague references to Judeo-Christian truth.

Native Andeans were selective in their adoption of Spanish customs and tried to maintain as many of their cherished beliefs as they could. They were accustomed to having foreign gods forced upon them and to incorporating them into their pantheon, for the Incas had been as energetic as the Spaniards in this practice.

Andeans interpreted Christianity in their own way, blending it into their own beliefs, and adapting to incorporate the new 'faith'. The outcome was an 'Andean Catholicism' that persists to the present day. In this way Andeans are 'dual citizens' in the worlds of the past and the present.

Despite great changes in Andean culture during the 500 years after the Spanish Conquest, much of Andean life remains inspired by the ancient concepts of exchange, collectivity, transformation and essence.

Left: An eighteenth-century Spanish colonial Corpus Christi procession. The bearing of the figure on a litter may be a vestige of Inca ancestor worship.

THE MEETING OF TWO GREAT FAITHS

When the Incas were expanding their empire, they had insisted that the state cult of Inti become part of the religion of their subjects. However, ancient Andean religious belief had always had many gods, not just one: there was an overarching creator god (with several regional names), but also many local gods. Belief in the entire landscape as sacred could not deny the relevance of local gods in the development of pre-Inca cultures. So the Incas tried to incorporate all these gods into their cult rather than to exclude them, and to show that the ancient ways and legends were, in fact, part of their own inheritance, and that they were merely the final arbiters.

When their fortunes changed with the arrival of Francisco Pizarro, however, it was the turn of the Incas to be converted. Attempts to convert them and their subject peoples began with Father Valverde, the friar who accompanied Francisco Pizarro

Below: This engraving fancifully depicts an offering to Inti, the Inca sun god. The kneeling man may represent a Catholic priest.

on his expedition against Atahualpa. Feigning peace, Pizarro had instructed Valverde to approach Atahualpa brandishing a crucifix and a Bible as they entered the main courtyard of Cajamarca on 15 November 1532. Valverde delivered a speech on Christianity. His words, translated by an interpreter, were said to be understood by Atahualpa, though we can never be sure. Atahualpa certainly understood what he was being asked to do – forsake his own god for another – for when Valverde handed him the Bible he threw it to the ground and replied, pointing at the sun, 'My god still lives.' This declaration refers to the cult of the Sapa Inca, who, as representative and son of Inti, the sun, was worshipped as a deity.

THE CULT OF VIRACOCHA

Before the Inca state cult transferred its focus to the sun god Inti, Viracocha had been the centre of attention and worship. Yet the antiquity and history of the cult of Viracocha is open to debate. What seems clear is that the Inca Viracocha was a combination of elements. The legend of

Above: Father Valverde, presumably appalled, had his Bible defiled when Atahualpa allegedly threw it to the ground.

his wanderings gives him the full names of Con Tici (Ticci, Titi or Ticsi) Viracocha Pachayachachic, or Coniraya Viracocha, sometimes including Illya. *Con* was the name of a central coastal creator deity. *Tici* is foundation, beginning or cause. *Ticsi* refers to crystal, *illya* to light. *Pacha* is an element in another coastal creator god, Pachacamac, meaning the universe, time and space. Finally, *yachachic* means teacher.

Viracocha's temple in Cuzco was at Quishuarcancha. Father Bernabé Cobo records that it contained a golden statue of him in human form about the size of a 10-year-old boy. Another Viracocha image was made of textiles and kept in the Temple of the Sun in the Coricancha.

The rise to dominance of Inti over Viracocha occurred during the 15th century, when there was a power struggle in Cuzco. The dispute was between the Inca

Above: The Spaniards symbolically built the Church of Santo Domingo on the foundations of the Inca sacred Coricancha.

ruler Viracocha (and his chosen heir Inca Urco) and Inca Pachacuti, another of his sons. The history was about 100 years old when Pizarro arrived, and details were obscured by time and by the Incas' obsession with having an official version for the new ruler. However, it cannot be coincidental that Viracocha had the name of the deity ultimately to be displaced and that his supplanter's name was the Quechua word for the revolution of the cycle of time! It was Pachacuti Inca Yupanqui who initiated the installation of the sun cult of Inti and began the rebuilding of Cuzco, the Coricancha Temple and the great Sun Temple of Sacsahuaman.

Among ordinary people the cult of Viracocha was not nearly so prominent as the worship of local deities, especially mountain deities and the earth deity Pacha Mama. The original derivation of *vira* and *cocha* can be traced to Aymara in the Titicaca Basin. In fact, Viracocha became a term used to refer to Spaniards and Christians in general and today is an honorific name for Westerners.

JESUS THE SUN
The Andean equation of Jesus Christ with the sun began in the early colonial period, an association that conformed to their 'former' belief that the Sapa Inca was the son of the sun and their association of Viracocha, creator of the sun and the moon, with Inti. The Christian god and the sun were both celestial deities and their conceptualization was similar.

The sun cult was revived in the 20th century. Today the sun is addressed as Huayna Capac (Young Lord), Hesu Kristu (Jesus Christ), Inti Tayta (Father Sun) and Taytacha (also Jesus Christ), a perfect combination of celestial deity, sun, and father and son.

The equation of the Virgin Mary with Pacha Mama is also colonial. Mary is linked to the moon through the moon's intimate association with the earth and its annual cycles through the agricultural year. The association is most prominent in August, at crop planting. In September the ritual of Coya Raymi (the empress's feast) is held to celebrate its successful completion. The moon is addressed as Mama Quilla (Mother Moon). Women take the active role and issue invitations to men to participate. Women's interest in the crops continues to the December solstice, when young boys take over care of the growing crops and the festival of Capac Raymi is held in honour of the sun.

SHARED BELIEFS
Christian missionaries saw elements in Inca belief that convinced them that they were merely 'lost children' of Christ. Indeed, many Andean religious concepts and Christian beliefs are superficially similar. The Andean concept of dualism – oneness within two – is not unlike the Judeo-Christian trinitarian belief of one within three.

The ultimate creator god Viracocha was a rather remote, overarching deity whose omnipresence was similar to the concept of God the Father. Viracocha's pervading presence throughout the universe was an omnipresent force, not an idol (although, like Christ, he was represented on Earth). Inca stories of a flood and of a single man and woman as progenitors of the human race could be perceived as the essence of Christian truth, if slightly corrupted by the passage of time and errors in record.

The biblical story of creation, in which humans began on earth with a man and a woman created by the supreme deity, resembled Andean belief, which also included a flood that destroyed everything that went before. Plagues and divine retribution were familiar, and sacrifices and gifts to the gods – for example the mass sacrifice at Huaca de la Luna at

Below: In this version of Father Valverde's attempt to convert Atahualpa, Pizarro is depicted kneeling – an unlikely occurrence.

Cerro Blanco to alleviate the effects of an El Niño event – were familiar pleas to the supreme being for help in bearing life's daily burdens.

Similarly, the legend of the wandering beggar Viracocha – as Christ, Son of God, who walked upon the earth and taught the people – was reconciled and incorporated. The ability of Viracocha to walk on water convinced many that Jesus must have come to the New World, perhaps after his resurrection or in a second visitation.

Sacred places of worship were also a familiar idea, including wells, springs and the importance of water. The concept of pilgrimage to sacred sites had been an Andean practice from at least the Early Horizon Chavín Cult. Sacred places as repositories for relics were everywhere in the Andean countryside and in villages, towns and cities. Christian worship and attribution of miraculous powers to saints' bones and pieces of the cross was recognizable.

FAMILIAR BELIEFS

Saints' feast days are celebrated with dances, the performers wearing masks to impersonate saints, much as the ancient Moche blood-sacrifice figures wore deity masks. A stone statue of Viracocha made by the Canas peoples of Cacha in the image of a Spanish priest in long white robes, and Viracocha's calling out of the ancestors, were attributed to the Titicaca Basin deity Tunapa, whom the native chronicler Pachacuti Yamqui believed to be Saint Thomas. Another native chronicler, Guamon Poma, believed Viracocha was Saint Bartholomew.

SHARED SYMBOLS

Ancient Andeans were also comfortable with much of Christian symbolism. Worship involved sacred objects: the cross, the chalice, candles and sacred vestments. The creed was 'kept' and recorded in the Bible. God was the creator and his

son was Jesus, who walked the earth and taught. Drugs were used: incense and wine in ceremony and sacred acts. And there was sacrifice, the crucifixion of Jesus Christ, a concept definitely familiar to ancient Andeans.

FINDING COMMON GROUND

Like the Incas, Christian preachers were willing to 'bend' a little in their efforts to convince themselves that their New World

Above: Ancient Andeans would have recognized the concept of human sacrifice but have had difficulty with the victim being described as the god himself.

converts' beliefs proved that Christian religion had been witnessed throughout the world – that things were always as they were in their Christian world. However, the recorders were the Spaniards themselves, and they were inclined to alter the stories they were told to fit preconceived ideas. For example, the three Viracochas (Con Tici, Imaymana and Tocapo) were a perfect triad that could be equated with the Holy Trinity, but what sixteenth-century Spanish priests did not know was that triadism is a concept in many cultures in the world.

In Andean triadism the kin-relationship of father and two sons, or three brothers, is less important than the structure of one principal and two helpers. This form is present in cult histories throughout the Andes. In some versions there is a fourth figure, Taguapaca, who disobeyed the father's instructions and was thrown into the River Desaguadero for his disobedience – the perfect foil of evil destroyed to leave the three principals of the narrative.

One of the ways in which Andean belief has survived is by being combined with Christianity. Some combinations were

Below: This puma devouring sinners was an attempt to seduce Native Americans into Christian belief using an Andean symbol.

Right: The Virgin Mary here remarkably resembles an Inca mummy bundle, and even has a staff-holding Inca depicted on her gown.

deliberate, as Spanish priests tried to ease the acceptance of Christianity. Much else was a natural blending of the Andeans' own beliefs with Christian ones: for example the sun is merged with Jesus, the Virgin Mary with Pacha Mama (the earth goddess) and Saint James of Santiago with Illapa.

IMPORTANT DIFFERENCES

Belief in an afterlife is a universal religious concept, though the idea that one's conduct on Earth was partly responsible for the nature of the afterlife was less entrenched in Andean belief. The difference was the Andean concept of *pachacuti*: a great cycle that repeated endlessly through time. Suffering was here on Earth, and the final journey of the spirit after physical death was allied to the Andean concept of essence, and the idea that death was the ultimate stage in life's cycle, with no thought of rebirth.

The concept of a second coming was embraced in Inkarrí, but is fundamentally more concerned with the return of the Incas to their rightful place in the scheme of things, their ingrained belief in *pachacuti* and a destiny to rule, rather than the Christian concept of Christ's return.

Spanish priests were unable to suppress the Inca solar cult: it survived in the central highlands and to the coast at Pachacamac. The sun continued to be a principal deity superior to mountain protector-guardian deities, and two aspects were recognized as daytime-sun, in the sky, and night-time sun, which travelled through the earth overnight. Throughout the highlands, the cults of Inti and Punchao (daytime sun) survived into colonial times and were associated with maize and the potato. In the 1560s a messianic movement called Taqui Onqoy (dancing sickness) revived the ancient *huacas* of Titicaca, Pachacamac and others,

perhaps eschewing the sun as associated with the Inca elite, who had been overpowered by the Spaniards.

Ultimately, ancient Andean beliefs could not be reconciled with Christian ones. The connections and parallels were too vague, and there were too many variations in Andean belief. Although there are undoubtedly similarities, they are merely superficial, for the concept of one god was fundamentally alien to ancient Andeans. However, Andeans were happy to keep their ancient religious ideas alongside Christianity, as long as they didn't have to give them up entirely. Thus, the Incas remained true to their belief in an established cycle of life in which they were at the cusp, destined to rule in the name of Inti. They were following the path that was ordained, fulfilling their destiny. Of course, the Spanish conquistadors held a similar belief, but they were conquering in the name of *their* god.

SACRED LOCATIONS

Reverence for sacred locations has never abated in Andean belief. From the powers of mountain gods and Pacha Mama to household deities such as Ekkeko, Andeans believe that offerings to such 'gods' can bring good fortune.

Spanish priests and administrators, focusing on conversion and on the elimination of ancestor cults, only slowly realized the tenacity with which Andean peoples stuck to their essential belief in the sacredness of the local landscape. Such beliefs go back to the foundations of the earliest cultures of the Andes and the first architectural ceremonial centres that mimicked the shapes of the landscape. The destruction of cult objects could not weaken such beliefs.

Andeans continue to regard identifiable stones or rock outcrops near their towns as characters from legendary scenes who have been turned to stone.

The ancient site of Pachacamac is perhaps the most ancient pilgrimage site in use. It persisted in colonial times as a

Below: Tens of thousands of people participate annually in the El Calvario ritual, merging Christian belief and sacred places.

sacred place. The Señor de los Milagros, or Crito Morado, here filled the place of the pre-Hispanic cult. Modern Peruvians visit Pachacamac to make offerings, especially to Pacha Mama.

HOUSEHOLD DEITIES

Ekkeko is a case in point. An Aymara deity dating from the Middle Horizon Tiwanaku culture, he was incorporated into Inca religion. Ekkeko household deity figures persisted through colonial times and are kept in households today to bring good luck. They are offered everything from coca leaves to Coca Cola in asking them to bring the household good fortune. The presence of Ekkeko makes every household a 'sacred place'. The use of such deity figures spread in the 1970s to many countries well beyond the Bolivian Altiplano.

Similarly, Inca stone and metal sculptures of plants and animals were considered repositories of health and powers for well-being. They were placed at *huacas* throughout the land. Today, Andeans keep small stones that either resemble animals or plants or have been carved to do so. Known as *inqa, inqaychu,*

Above: Shrines remained sacred to the Inca. The seated-puma-shaped rock at Qenqo continued to remind the Incas of Viracocha.

conopa or *illa*, they are believed to be gifts from mountain *apus*. Some have been passed down through many generations. Modern versions can be miniature plastic trucks, rubber sandals, cans of drink, money or even passports, and they can be bought at pilgrimage sites before being offered to local deities or saints.

Taking an object that belonged to a deceased important person in one's *ayllu* kinship group to that person's favourite place would invoke the person's memory among his descendants and also enhance the power of the sacred place. The act was not merely repetitious, but was meant to build the kin-group's history and link it through time to the present.

HUACA SHRINES

The royal *panaca* and sacred *huacas* of the Inca emperors were especially important to kin-group history. As part of the cult of the Sapa Inca as Inti's representative on earth, when Tupa Yupanqui died, his son Huana Capac visited the places

Above: The Qoyllur Rit'i ritual, begun after an alleged 18th-century miracle, revives the ancient Andean concept of ritual procession.

his father liked best, especially in Cajamarca, and built shrines at them. One tradition in the history of Inca origins describes Mount Huanacauri as the 'father' of the three founding ancestors, who were turned into stone around Cuzco. Even today, some Andeans regard local *huacas* in their region 'like parents'. Such places were believed to have given rise to their ancestors, and local caves were often where Andeans stored the mummified remains of ancestors until they were destroyed in colonial times by the Spaniards. Substantial evidence for

Below: This Qoyllur Rit'i procession is to the sacred Mt Sinakara, where Mariano herded his llamas and met the mestizo boy.

provincial shrine systems like those around Cuzco – for example colonial records – is sparse, however, and probably awaits discovery by ethnohistorians.

QOYLLUR RIT'I

One of the most celebrated 'modern' festivals involving place is Qoyllur Rit'i in the southern Andes, attended annually by tens of thousands of people. Held during the three weeks leading to the feast of Corpus Christi, the ritual is focused on several sanctuaries around Ocongate. Costumed dancers perform in honour of 'El Señor'.

The ritual is a typical mixture of ancient and Christian beliefs. The object of devotion is an image of Christ that miraculously appeared on a rock: El Señor de Qoyllur Rit'i (Lord of the Snow Star). The ritual began in the late 18th century, when the Catholic authorities replaced an indigenous cult with a Christian shrine. The Catholic Church officially accepted the miraculous appearance of Christ's image.

The ancient cult associated Ocongate as a venue of worship at the transition and regeneration of the new year. The blending of Christian and ancient belief revolves around the miracle in which a young llama herder, Mariano, encountered a mestizo boy on Mount Sinakara. Mariano was cold and hungry and the other boy shared his food. Mariano's herd increased and his father offered him new clothes as a reward. Mariano asked for new clothes for his friend too. He took the mestizo boy's

poncho to market to have it duplicated. The Bishop of Cuzco noted the old poncho's fine material and asked Mariano about the mestizo. Church officials sent to meet him encountered him wearing a white tunic, surrounded by a blinding radiance emanating from a silhouette When one official tried to touch it, he grasped a *tayanka* bush, above which, on a rock, appeared the image of Christ crucified. Mariano fell dead and was buried at the foot of the rock where the image appeared. A chapel was built to house the Tanyaka Cross and Mariano's sepulchre. Christ Tanyaka is believed to have been transformed into the rock, and the Catholic Church later had Christ's image painted on the rock-face.

Below: Husband and wife believers burn incense and make an offering to Pacha Mama in a ceremony in the La Paz Valley.

PROCESSIONS, FESTIVALS AND RITES

Architectural forms and sculptures in mud plaster and stone show that processions, ritual festivals and sacred rites were a part of ancient Andean culture.

ANCIENT PROCESSIONS

Ancient Andeans were intimately familiar with the concept of sacred routes. Cuzco alone had more than 300 sacred shrines along sacred *ceque* routes, ranging from monumental buildings to natural features. So important were processional routes to the Incas that archaeologists project their use to as far back as the Initial Period, suggesting that processions through U-shaped ceremonial precincts proceeded down into and through sunken courts, back out of them, and up on to temple platforms mimicking mountains, to honour earth and sky deities.

The established purpose of the famous Nazca desert lines – geoglyphs – was for ritual processions that followed the course of the lines. Geoglyphs of animals, birds or geometric patterns consist of a single line that never crosses itself. There are also nodes from which lines radiate.

The tradition of *ceque* routes made Christian processional routes, such as the Stations of the Cross, easy to comprehend.

Below: The 'festival' of Inti Raymi, the Inca June/winter solstice, attracts large crowds and is taken seriously to revive ancient Inca pageantry at the shrine of Sacsahuaman.

Left: The Nazca even made clay models of ancient processions, including a central shaman.

Pilgrimage to holy shrines was also a common ancient Andean practice. Similarly, ancient Andean sacrificial practices made recognition of the apparent ritual execution of Christ a familiar concept.

The Qoyllur Rit'i ritual involves processions by two groups representing the warm lands of the north-west (from Paucartambo town) and the colder pasture land of the south-east (from Quispicanchis town). The procession represents ancient Andean regional opposition and mutual exchange, and even linguistic dualism, for the Paucartambos are Quechua speakers while the Quispicanchis speak Aymara.

FEAST DAYS

Just as early Christians in a pagan Europe adapted and combined many feast days and ceremonies into the Christian calendar as their religion spread, so Christian Andeans have equated many ancient Andean ceremonial days to established Christian dates.

The recitation of the myth-histories of founding ancestors in provincial communities was made at annual high points such as planting (Pocoymita) and harvesting (Caruaymita), both of which became associated with Christian holy days. Ancient Andeans began to harvest their various crops in mid-April, and finished the collection and storage of produce by early June. These activities coincided with the disappearance of the Pleiades constellation in the night sky in April and its June reappearance above the horizon. The Pleiades were called *collca* ('storehouse') by the Incas, and ancient Andeans regarded it as the celestial container of the essence of all agricultural produce. With the arrival of Christianity, the movable feast of Corpus Christi soon became equated with the rising of the Pleiades at the same time as the rising of the sun.

Festivals mixing ancient Andean ritual with Christian practice and dates are those of Capac Raymi (December summer solstice) and Inti Raymi (June winter solstice), and the revival of the ritual re-enactment of the founding of Cuzco by Manco Capac, celebrated annually.

Such rituals can be regarded as a rejuvenation of ancient belief and power, which would have been understandable

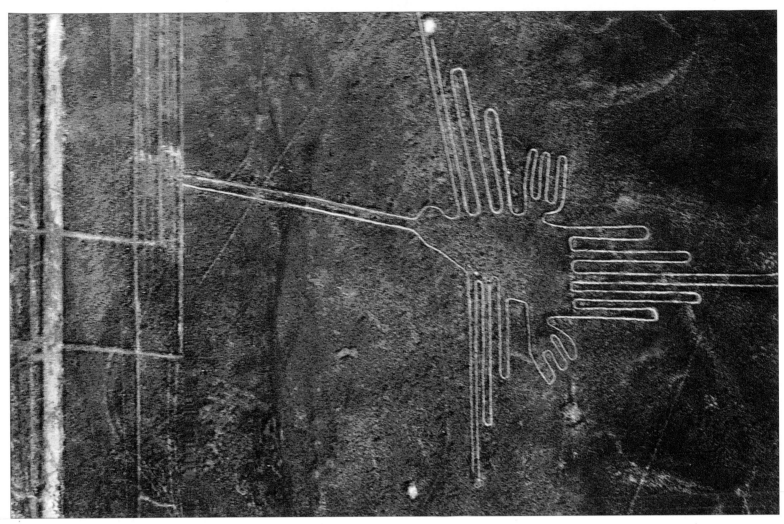

Above: Humming bird in the Nazca desert. Geoglyph lines were thought of as processional pathways, perhaps 'owned' by kin groups.

in an atmosphere and perception of powerlessness against hundreds of years of colonial oppression.

DEEDS OF THE ANCESTORS

When the first Spaniards entered Cuzco they witnessed the arrangement of the mummified Inca emperors in the main plaza. The keepers of Inca history, the *amautas* and *harahuicus*, were responsible for collating the histories and deeds of the emperors. On ritual occasions, it was their task to recite these histories in the forms of short stories by the former and poems by the latter, incorporating stylistic devices such as set speeches, repeated metaphor and refrains intentionally reshaped and elaborated from one performance to the next.

Occasions for such performances included the initiation rites of teenage boys as adults during the month leading up to Capac Raymi (late November–December), the summer solstice. The boys visited the peaks in the southern Cuzco Valley where the Inca ancestors stopped on their route to Cuzco. Other occasions were at the celebration of military victories, royal successions and, of course, royal funerals.

It was Inca Pahcacuti, religious reformer and initiator of the cult of Inti, who ordered that 'songs' (*cantares* in the Spanish chronicles) were sung by the attendants of the imperial 'statues' (ancestor mummies and *huauques*) at 'fiestas'. The performance began with the deeds of Manco Capac, the founder ancestor, and proceeded through the emperors up to the reigning Sapa Inca. Colonial records describe such performances of myth-histories in provincial centres as well.

STAMPING OUT IDOLATRY

Priests and Spanish administrators fought a continuing battle against what they regarded as idolatry, as manifested in the cults and virtual worship of the mummified remains of *ayllu* founders and ancestors. They ruthlessly hunted down and tried the perpetrators of ancestor cults and burned their mummified ancestors, until by the end of the 16th century all were destroyed.

In the eyes of the Incas, the Spaniards were equally wicked in their treatment of Inti. The great golden sun disc that hung in the Coricancha had been awarded to one of the conquistadors, who promptly gambled it away in a late-night card game – thus the Andean expression 'to gamble the sun before dawn'.

REVIVALS

Many Inca rites and processions have been revived, especially in the late 20th century. Based, as were their ancestors, primarily on an agricultural way of life, Native South American descendants and mestizos seek to alleviate the hardships of life by continuing to honour traditional belief in the sacredness of the land of their forefathers and to reconcile this with modern life.

ANIMISM AND COCA

Animism was fundamental in ancient Andean religion: the forces of nature were and are believed to be 'living beings' that affect life. Humans were only one group of beings among animals and plants. The images of supernatural beings based on living animals, such as the jaguar, snakes, predatory birds and spiders, and the depiction of transformation, reveal such belief. Animals were thought to possess powers and wisdom that could benefit humans, and certain humans, the shamans, were capable of shape-shifting to become, temporarily, the animal in question and take on the animal's nature.

Below: This Moche spouted vessel displays an intoxicated shaman, holding his wooden stick and coca container to make coca balls.

THE LIVING EARTH

Agriculture was fundamental to ancient Andean civilization and still forms the basis of most of Andean society. Agricultural fertility is therefore deeply ingrained in the Andean psyche, and with it worship of Pacha Mama – the living earth – and the natural elements. Ceremonial rites to Pacha Mama, the matrix for all life, continue to be performed regularly throughout the year, highlighted on important dates in agriculture, and also when visiting sacred places and at the start of a long journey. At harvest ceremonies, young women impersonate Pacha Mama Suyrumama by wearing long red dresses ('mother earth of the long dress that drags along the ground').

The field called Ayllipampa, near Cuzco, is dedicated to Pacha Mama. Bernabé Cobo described how farmers worshipped her at stone altars containing miniature women's clothing in the middle of the field. Other deities associated with Pachcmama are Mama Oca, Mama Coca and Mama Sara (Maize Mother). Central Andeans continue to maintain that the Inca ancestress Mama Huaco, who sowed the first maize field, and others sustain the agricultural well-being of the community. The field of Sausero outside Cuzco was dedicated to her.

Agricultural ferility is also believed to be affected by mountain *apu* deities and celestial gods, including Illapa (lightning and thunder), Cuichu (rainbow) and Ccoa (a supernatural feline who causes destructive hail).

THE POWER OF *CHICHA*

Today, rural *ayllus* continue to plough and plant communal fields at festivals. There are contests to see who can work fastest at ploughing and planting the largest amount of land. Festive meals are served, accompanied by plenty of *chicha* or maize beer. There are *chicha* libations and offerings of coca to Pacha Mama, the community ancestors and the local

Above: Continuing ancient practice, a modern Peruvian makes an offering of coca leaves to a local deity or saint.

sacred places, alongside Christian prayers to the community's patron saints, who seem to have taken the place of the ancestors.

Llamas are ritually honoured in August. They are force-fed a *chicha*, barley and herbal mash to intoxicate them before being released on to the Altiplano, followed by their equally intoxicated herders singing and playing flutes. Such ritual drunkenness is believed to enhance fertility. Libations are poured to invite Pacha Mama and the *apus* to the celebrations. Intoxication also blurs the distinction between humans, animals and the landscape as they all 'dance together'.

SACRIFICE BEHIND THE ALTAR

Ancient sacrifices and offerings continued in secrecy well into Spanish colonial times. Although known as the 'sacrifice behind the altar' syndrome, this is not

to be taken literally, as the sacrifices and offerings simply occurred in remote places away from churches. Animal sacrifices, together with offerings of agricultural produce and coca, and the burning of incense with prayers are still practised, often alongside offerings of modern 'western' products such as cigarettes and Coca Cola, and also often in connection with Christian ceremonies.

Left: A silver figurine depicts a woman with puffed cheeks, chewing a coca wad, which induces stamina and suppresses hunger.

Mountains (especially volcanoes), caves and springs remain particularly sacred. Mountains continue to be regarded as the dwelling places of the ancestral dead.

The fundamental Andean cosmological frame remains an anchor to Andean society: the sun rises over the sacred mountains in the east, brings life, and sets in the west, the final resting place of the dead.

SHAMANS

Local shamanism also still has an important place in local communities. For everyday illnesses, many Andeans consult their local *curandero*, a person skilled in the use of herbs and potions, harking back to the 5th-century AD Wari cave burial of a herbalist. Shaman-curers were frequently depicted in Moche and other effigy vessels.

Cures include the use of water and perfume exhaled over a (looted) skull from a pre-Hispanic burial, in the belief that the spirit of the deceased person will protect the afflicted as well as the curer from evil interventions. Potent hallucinogenic mescaline brews are still made from the San Pedro cactus. Chants and prayers used in such cures are a mixture

Above: Native South Americans and cholos (people of Spanish descent) in a Christian-native ceremony at El Calvario, Bolivia.

of pre-Hispanic and Christian practices. Sticks, which represent swords, are used to fight with the spirits of 'the other world' and keep them from harming the patient. As in ancient times, the shaman acts as an intermediary between the human and spirit worlds.

COCA

The regular chewing of coca leaves continues as a stimulant and aid in coping with the harsh climate and high Andean altitudes. The Spaniards quickly learned its properties of keeping otherwise exhausted labourers and miners energized, and exploited its perceived sacred symbolic power as, once again, their Christian convictions were compromised by practical needs. Coca cultivation increased under Spanish rule. Coca leaves are a frequent offering to Pacha Mama especially, and there is irony in their 'integration' from ancient use to modern times, for the leaf is referred to as Hostia (the Host) and its ritual consumption compared to Holy Communion.

Coca remains a major part of the Andean indigenous economy and is, of course, exploited internationally in its refinement for the drug trade.

THE RETURN OF THE INCAS

Twentieth-century social studies of Andean culture have discovered an underlying theme that represents a source of post-Conquest cross-Andean unity: the theme of the dying and reviving Inca, as encapsulated in the legend of Inkarrí.

THE FIVE AGES

A late Inca cosmology comprised a five-age sequence of the creation of the Inca world. The First Age was ruled by Viracocha and the other gods, and death was unknown. The Second Age was that of the giants created by Viracocha, who worshipped him but who displeased him and were destroyed by a flood. The Third Age was inhabited by the first humans, again created by Viracocha, but they lived on a primitive level and lacked even the rudiments of civilization. The Fourth Age was that of the *Auca Runa* ('the warriors'), to whom Viracocha presumably imparted the arts of civilization, for these were the creators of the early civilizations such as the Moche and the Tiwanaku.

Below: After unsuccessful revolts against Spanish rule, the legend grew that the Incas retreated east into the rainforest to Paititi.

The Fifth Age was that of the Incas themselves, who spread civilization far and wide through conquest. The Fifth Age ended with the coming of the Spaniards and with the downfall of the Inca Empire, but upon their arrival the Spaniards were hailed as the returning emissaries of the creator and were referred to as *viracochas* – a term still used as one of respect.

THE STORY OF INKARRÍ

Inkarrí is the central character in a post-Spanish Conquest Inca millenarian belief in the 'dying and reviving Inca'. The derivation of the name itself is a combination of the Quechua word *Inca* and the Spanish word *rey*, both meaning 'king' or 'ruler'. The legend foretells a time when the current sufferings of the original peoples of the Andes will be ended in a cataclysmic transformation of the world, in which the Spanish overlords will be destroyed. The true Inca will be resurrected and reinstated in his rightful place as supreme ruler, and prosperity and justice will be returned to the world.

A typical example of one of the versions of the Inkarrí myth recounts how Inkarrí was the son of a savage woman

Above: A modern Peruvian impersonates the Sapa Inca at the festival of Inti Raymi. It is believed that the emperor will one day return.

and Father Sun. Inkarrí was powerful. He harnessed the sun, his father, and the very wind itself. He drove stones with a whip, ordered them around, and founded a city called K'ellk'ata, probably Cuzco. Then he threw a golden rod from a mountaintop, but found that the city did not fit on the plain where it landed, so he moved the city to its present location. When the Spaniards arrived, however, they imprisoned Inkarrí in a secret place, and his head is all that remains. However, Inkarrí is growing a new body and will return when he is whole again.

PACHACUTI

Belief in the return of Inkarrí is clearly in keeping with the Andean concept of *pachacuti*, the revolution or reversal of time and space. It arose from the native populations' sense that the Spaniards had created oppression and injustice. It may hark back to events of the first few

Right: Tupac Amaru, the 'last Inca emperor', was beheaded in Cuzco's central plaza. His head was spirited away and secretly buried.

decades after the Spanish Conquest, in which the last Inca emperor, Atahualpa, was believed to have been beheaded by Francisco Pizarro shortly after his defeat, and to the beheading of Tupac Amaru, a claimant to the Inca throne, who led an unsuccessful revolt against Spanish rule in the 1560s and 1570s. In different accounts, the two heads were taken to Lima or to Cuzco, but in both cases the belief is that, once buried in the ground, the head becomes a seed that rejoins its body in anticipation of return.

THE RETURN TO CUZCO

Another belief concerns the removal of Inca power to a hidden land. The legend records that upon being expelled from Cuzco the Incas travelled east through the mountains. They built bridges as they went, but they placed enchantments on

Below: The retreating Incas built enchanted bridges as they went, so that their route could not be followed.

their route so that no one could follow. If they did, the enchantment caused them to fall asleep on the spot for ever.

The Incas travelled across the mountains into the jungle and established a hidden city called Paititi. Here they remain in hiding. 'Foreigners' who seek Paititi can never find it. One found a talking bridge; when he tried to cross it, he was chased away by huge felines and *amarus* (mythical serpent-dragons) guarding the bridge.

According to the legend, *pachacuti* will turn and the Inca will return, following the route they used when they left Cuzco. There will be tremendous hail and lightning, wind and earthquakes. *Amarus* will roar from mountains and mestizos will be chased away. When the Incas return they will recognize only their *runakuna* descendants, who wear traditional llama-wool clothing, and the Incas will assume their rightful place and rule again.

GLOSSARY

acllas chosen women, picked to serve in the state cult of Inti

acllahuasi special buildings where *acllas* were housed

amarus mythical serpent-dragons

amautas also *harahuicus* Inca record-keepers

andones hillside terraces

apacheta special type of *huaca* – a stone cairn on a mountain pass or at a crossroads

apu sacred deity who lives on a mountain top, or the mountain top itself

aridenes cultivation terraces

atl-atl spear thrower

auca treasonous enemy of the state

audiencias small divisions within Chan Chan *ciudadela*

ayar legendary ancestors of the Incas

ayllu a kinship group or division with mutual obligations to other *ayllus*

ayni the principle that governed cyclicity

capacocha specially selected sacrificial victim

ceque sighting line or sacred pathway leading from Cuzco

chachapuma puma-headed person

chicha beer made from maize

chullpa tower where the Colla people put mummified remains, and into which more could be added

ciudadela Chimú walled compound at Chan Chan

collca storehouse

curaca leader/official

curandero person skilled in the use of herbs and potions

hanan upper

huaca sacred place – a natural, man-made or modified natural feature

huaca adatorio sanctuary or temple

huaca sepultura burial place of the most important deceased individuals

huanca stone(s) regarded as the petrified ancestor of a people or *apu*

huauques man-made statues – doubles – made in the image of the ruling Sapa Incas and other chiefs and nobles during their lifetimes

hurin lower

idolatrías Spanish Colonial documents written as reports of the Spaniards'

investigations of idolatrous practices among the native peoples

inqa (also *inqaychu*, *conopa* or *illa*) small stones that either resemble animals or plants or have been carved to do so, believed to be gifts from mountain *apus*

intihuatana a 'hitching post of the sun' – special *huaca* of Inti

kalanka rectangular hall used for public functions

kancha residential building

kero a drinking cup, especially for *chicha*, made from wood, pottery, gold or silver

mallquis mummified founding ancestor, Inca emperor or local leader

mama female

mit'a labour service/tax

mitamaes peoples redistributed within an empire

mitamaq the redistribution of people

montaña forested slopes of the Andes

moza commoner/outsider

napa miniature llama figurine

pacarina the place of origin, the place from which one's ancestors (one's tribe, nation or *ayllu* kinship group) emerged

pachacuti a turning over/revolution/a cycle of the world

pampa vast prairie in South America south of the Amazon

panaca kinship group; the royal panaca was the Inca *ayars*

plazas hundidas plazas or sunken courts

puna sierra basin or valley

qhaqha person or animal killed by lightning

quipu system of knotted bundles of string of different colours, used for recording information

quipucamayoqs knot-makers (i.e. makers and keepers of *quipus*)

runakuna Inca descendants who wear traditional llama-wool clothing

runaquipu-camayoc a census recorder

suyu quarter of the Inca Empire

tambo a way-station, which was used to accommodate pilgrims

tocoyrikoq provincial governor

topacusi golden cup or vessel

tumbaga amalgamated precious metals

tumi crescent-shaped knife used for ritual bloodletting or decapitation

wasi covered chamber

yanacona a selected court retainer

yaya male

INDEX

I would like to dedicate this book to my wife Anne, daughter Megan and son Sam.

This edition is published by Lorenz Books, an imprint of Anness Publishing Ltd, Hermes House, 88–89 Blackfriars Road, London SE1 8HA; tel. 020 7401 2077; fax 020 7633 9499

www.lorenzbooks.com; www.annesspublishing.com

Anness Publishing has a new picture agency outlet for images for publishing, promotions or advertising. Please visit our website www.practicalpictures.com for more information.

UK agent: The Manning Partnership Ltd; tel. 01225 478444; fax 01225 478440; sales@manning-partnership.co.uk
UK distributor: Grantham Book Services Ltd; tel. 01476 541080; fax 01476 541061; orders@gbs.tbs-ltd.co.uk
North American agent/distributor: National Book Network; tel. 301 459 3366; fax 301 429 5746; www.nbnbooks.com
Australian agent/distributor: Pan Macmillan Australia; tel. 1300 135 113; fax 1300 135 103; customer.service@macmillan.com.au
New Zealand agent/distributor: David Bateman Ltd; tel. (09) 415 7664; fax (09) 415 8892

Publisher: Joanna Lorenz
Senior Managing Editor: Conor Kilgallon
Editor: Joy Wotton
Designers: Nigel Partridge and Adelle Morris
Illustrators: Anthony Duke, Rob Highton and Vanessa Card
Editorial Reader: Lindsay Zamponi
Production Controller: Steve Lang

ETHICAL TRADING POLICY
Because of our ongoing ecological investment programme, you, as our customer, can have the pleasure and reassurance of knowing that a tree is being cultivated on your behalf to naturally replace the materials used to make the book you are holding. For further information about this scheme, go to www.annesspublishing.com/trees

© Anness Publishing Ltd 2007

PICTURE ACKNOWLEDGEMENTS
The Ancient Art and Architecture Collection: 5.5, 6bl, 8bl, 25tl, 25br, 37bl, 65bl, 81, 82bl, 90bl, 93bm, 111tl, 119tr, 153tr, 160bl, 161bl, 163tl, 191tr, 214-215, 216tr, 223bl, 228tr.

The Art Archive: /Album/J. Enrique Molina: 204, 219t, 224bl, 233tr, /Alcazar, Seville/Dagli Orti: 12tr, /Amano Museum, Lima/Album/J. Enrique Molina: 234bl, /Amano Museum, Lima/Dagli Orti: 5br, 145tm, /Amano Museum, Lima/Mireille Vautier: 141bl, 224tr, /Archaeological Museum, Lima/Album/J. Enrique Molina: 220bl, /Archaeological Museum, Lima/Dagli Orti: 25tm, 78, 84, 85tm, 126–7, 132bl, 136bl, 142bl, 142tr, 147bm, 154bl, 179tr, 179bm, 180, 188bl, 217br, 229, 230bl, 244tr, /Archaeological Museum, Lima/Mireille Vautier: 135bl, 159bl, 203tr, 234tr, 246bl, /Archbishops Palace Museum, Cuzco/ Mireille Vautier: 210tl, /Arteaga Collection, Peru/Mireille Vautier: 151br, 210br, /Biblioteca Nazionale Marciana, Venice/Dagli Orti: 39tl, /Bibliotheque des Arts Decoratifs, Paris/Dagli Orti: 238bl, /Stephanie Colasanti: 160tr, 165tr, 169t, 211tm, 211br, 239tl, 244bl, /Dagli Orti: 4.4, 4.5, 5.1, 26tr, 44tr, 60bl, 74–5, 80bl, 88, 94-95, 102bl, 105tr, 114bl, 128-129, 133bl, 134tr, 135tr, 144tr, 150, 162bl, 162br, 166tl, 166tr, 169br, 170bl, 171bl, 172tr, 176tr, 177t, 178bl, 190, 192bl, 193bl, 195t, 200tr, 213br, 220tr, 242tr, /Chavez Ballon Collection, Lima/Mireille Vautier: 194tr, /Gold Museum, Lima/ Mireille Vautier: 185, /La Gringa Collection/Mireille Vautier: 137br, /Money Museum, Potosi, Bolivia/Mireille Vautier: 241tr, /Musee du Chateau de Versailles/Dagli Orti: 13tr, /Museo Banco de Guayaquil, Ecuador/Dagli Orti: 5.3, 174–5, /Museo Ciudad, Mexico/Dagli Orti: 18tr, /Museo de Arte Colonial de Santa Catalina, Cuzco/Dagli Orti: 240, /Museo de Arte Municipal, Lima/Dagli Orti: 231, /Museo del Banco Central de Reserva, Lima/Dagli Orti: 235bl, /Museo del Oro, Lima/Dagli Orti: 113bm, 134bl, 141tr, 221, 227br, 228bl, /Museo Nacional de Historica, Lima/Mireille Vautier: 249tr, /Museo Nacional Tiahuanacu, La Paz, Bolivia/Dagli Orti: 24ml, 120tr, /Museo Pedro de Osma, Lima/Dagli Orti: 5.6, 236–7, /Museo Pedro de Osma, Lima/Mireille Vautier: 27tr, 35tr, 106tr, 208tr, 209bl, /Museo Regional de Ica, Peru/Dagli Orti: 183, /Museum Larco Herra, Lima/Album/J. Enrique Molina: 178tm, /Navy Historical Service, Vincennes, France/Dagli Orti: 18bl, /Science Academy, Lisbon/ Dagli Orti: 15, /University Museum, Cuzco/Mireille Vautier: 36tr, 121br, 158bl, 159tr, 176bl, /Mireille Vautier: 227tl, 238tr, 247bl.

Andrew McLeod: 6tr, 25bl, 26tm, 27bm, 27br, 140tm, 161tr, 250tm, 252bm, 253bm, 255br, 255tr, 256br, 256tl.

Sally Phillips: 7bl, 25bm, 26br, 102tr, 158tr, 253tl, 254bl.

Frances Reynolds: 25tr, 26bl, 27tm, 27bl, 46tr, 47tl, 68tr, 107tr, 125br, 250br, 251tr.

Nick Saunders: 21tr, 26bm, 27tl, 35bl, 38bl, 58bl, 61bl, 62tr, 65tr, 70tr, 89tr, 117tl, 121t, 147tr, 156tr, 162tr, 164bl, 171tr, 173br, 186, 194bl, 198bl, 208bl, 222t, 225, 235tl, 241bl, 245.

South American Pictures: 12bl, 13bl, 14bl, 16bl, 31bl, 34tr, 36bl, 37tr, 39br, 40bl, 40tr, 41tr, 69tl, 72tr, 93tr, 107bl, 122bl, 124tr, 137tl, 192tr, 198tr, 199bl, 205bl, 219br, 226tr, 230tr, 233bl, 239br, 250bl, 251br, 252tl, 253tr, 254tm /Danny Aeberhard: 53tr, /Ann Bailetti: 116tr, /Phillipa Bowles: 59t, /Hilary Bradt: 73, /Britt Dyer: 62bl, /Robert Francis: 48tr, 87bl, 91bm, 112tr, /Steve Harrison: 55bl, /Jason P. Howe: 248tr, /Kathy Jarvis: 4.2, 4.3, 20tr, 22–3, 26tl, 33, 42–3, 44bl, 45tl, 56–7, 63br, 82tm, 82br, 83tl, 83br, 105bl, 143tr, 145br, /Joseph Martin: 38tr, /Kimball Morrison: 177br, /Marion Morrison: 60tr, 101br, 200bl, /Tony Morrison: 1, 2, 4br, 4.1, 5.4, 8tr, 9tl, 10-11, 14tr, 19bl, 19tr, 20bl, 21bl, 28-29, 30bl, 30tr, 32bl, 32tr, 34bl, 41b, 46bl, 47br, 47tr, 48bl, 49bl, 49tr, 50tr, 51bl, 52tr, 53bl, 54bl, 58tr, 59br, 61tr, 64bl, 66tr, 67tr, 71, 85bl, 85br, 86bl, 87tr, 89bl, 90tr, 91t, 92bl, 96, 98tr, 100tr, 101tl, 103br, 106b, 110tr, 111br, 113t, 114tr, 115br, 116bl, 117br, 118bl, 119bl, 123, 124bl, 130bl, 130tr, 131tr, 132tr, 138, 140b, 144bl, 146bl, 156bl, 157tl, 157br, 163br, 164tr, 165bl, 167tr, 167bl, 170bl, 173tl, 178br, 181b, 182bl, 184bl, 188tr, 191bl, 195bm, 196-197, 199tr, 201t, 202bl, 202tr, 203bl, 205tr, 206bl, 206tr, 207bl, 207tr, 212bl, 213tl, 216bl, 217tl, 222bm, 242bl, 243br, 246tr, 247tr, 248bl, 249bl, /Kim Richardson: 243t, 243bl, /Peter Ryley: 67bl, /Chris Sharp: 9br, 64tr, 77br, 99, 218tr, /Karen Ward: 55tr, 63tl.

Werner Forman Archive: 24tr, 122tr, 133tr, 139tl, /British Museum, London: 16tr, 68bl, 112bl, 139br, 154tr, / Dallas Museum of Art, Dallas: 3, 86tr, 87tl, 131bl, 223tr, /David Bernstein Collection, New York: 4.6, 108-109, 110bl, 118tr, 136bl, 146r, 152tr, 182tr, /Guggenheim Museum, New York: 54tr, /Maxwell Museum of Anthropology, Albuquerque, NM: 76bl, 77tl, /Museum fur Volkerkunde, Berlin: 17, 69br, 79tr, 100bl, 125tl, 153bl, 187bl, 189tl, 189br, 201bl, 218bl, 226bl, 232, 235br, /Private Collection: 5.2, 79bl, 148–9, 153br, 155bl, /Royal Museum of Art & History, Brussels: 184tr.

p.1 Carved Inca face. p. 2 Winay Wayna.
p.3 Moche effigy jar Above: Sacsayhuaman.
Left: Runkuaqay.